THE DIVIDED WORLD

THE DIVIDED WORLD

Human Rights and
Its Violence

RANDALL WILLIAMS

University of Minnesota Press
Minneapolis • London

The University of Minnesota Press gratefully acknowledges the work of Roderick A. Ferguson, editorial consultant, on this project.

Published by the University of Minnesota Press
111 Third Avenue South, Suite 290
Minneapolis, MN 55401-2520
http://www.upress.umn.edu

Library of Congress Cataloging-in-Publication Data

Williams, Randall, 1964–
    The divided world : human rights and its violence / Randall Williams
        p. cm.
    ISBN 978-0-8166-6541-9 (hc : alk. paper)
    ISBN 978-0-8166-6542-6 (pb : alk. paper)
    1. Human rights. 2. Political violence. I. Title.
    JC571.W7224 2010
    323′2 22   2009012625

Printed in the United States of America on acid-free paper

The University of Minnesota is an equal-opportunity educator and employer.

18 17 16 15 14 13 12 11 10   10 9 8 7 6 5 4 3 2 1

Yes, we are all human beings...
but some are sons of bitches
and some aren't.
That's the truth.

— Subcomandante Marcos

Contents

Acknowledgments

In a certain sense, this is the most difficult part of the book to write. So many people have done so much to make this work possible that I cannot begin to acknowledge them in any adequate manner. But here it goes: Rosaura Sánchez and Lisa Lowe for their unwavering support, intellectual guidance, and solid political commitments; my parents, Leota and Burl, for life, sustenance, and unconditional love; my brother Stan for forging a fiercely independent path for me to follow; Sandra Angeleri and Ricardo Bracho, my brilliant and beautiful ideological partners-in-crime; Helen Jun for the sheer fun of it all; and Stephen Wu for his boundless enthusiasm for all that is wondrous in the world.

Mentors and interlocutors: Barbara Harlow, David Lloyd, Inderpal Grewal, Lisa Yoneyama, Shelley Streeby, and Masao Miyoshi. *Comrades and confidants:* Albert Lowe, Amie Parry, Barry Masuda, Beatrice Pita, Ben Ehrenreich, Boone Nguyen, Chandan Reddy, David Hernandez, David Mueller, Denise Ferreira da Silva, Dylan Rodríguez, Ernest Hardy, Gerard Koskovich, Grace Hong, James Tobler, Jason Ortiz, Jennifer Sternad, Jodi Kim, Jorge Cortiñas, Keith Camacho, Keith Harris, Kevin Pimentel, Kulvinder Aurora, Lisa Cacho, Malik Dohrn, Miguel Gutierrez, Ofelia Cuevas, Pedro Bustos-Aguilar, Rubén Martínez, Ryan Kahl, Setsu Shigematsu, Spenger Charles, Tania Triana, Tede Matthews, Victor Bascara. *Publishers:* the talented and committed folks at the University of Minnesota Press, especially my astute and kind editor, Richard Morrison; editorial consultant Roderick Ferguson for getting behind this project; the anonymous readers who gave me excellent revision suggestions and more work to do; and John Eagleson for patiently pouring over every word. *Influences:* Everyone whose work is referenced in this book (and some who are not, but will be in the next one). Finally, *to all those past and present who have struggled, collectively and privately, for a different kind of world. Kayn, this includes you.*

Abbreviations

AI	Amnesty International
ALN	Armée de Libération Nationale (National Liberation Army, Algeria)
ANC	African National Congress
BIA	Board of Immigration Appeal (United States)
BPC	Black People's Convention (South Africa)
BWP	Black Workers Project (South Africa)
CCG	Círculo Cultural Gay (Gay Cultural Circle, Mexico)
CCRI	Comité Clandestino Revolucionario Indígena (Clandestine Revolutionary Indigenous Committee, Mexico)
ERP	Ejército Revolucionario del Pueblo (People's Revolutionary Army, Argentina)
EZLN	Ejército Zapatista de Liberación Nacional (Zapatista Army of National Liberation, Mexico)
FLN	Front de Libération Nationale (National Liberation Front, Algeria)
FSLN	Frente Sandinista de Liberación Nacional (Sandinista National Liberation Front, Nicaragua)
ICC	International Criminal Court
IGA	International Gay Association
ILGA	International Lesbian and Gay Association
ILGHRC	International Lesbian and Gay Human Rights Commission
INS	Immigration and Naturalization Service (United States)
NAMBLA	North American Man–Boy Love Association

NAYO	National Association of Youth Organizations (South Africa)
NGO	nongovernmental organization
OAS	Organization of American States
PAN	Partido Acción Nacional (National Action Party, Mexico)
POC	prisoner of conscience
PRD	Partido de la Revolución Democrática (Party of the Democratic Revolution, Mexico)
PRI	Partido Revolucionario Institucional (Institutional Revolutionary Party, Mexico)
SASM	South African Students Movement
UDF	United Democratic Front (South Africa)
UDHR	Universal Declaration of Human Rights
UNAM	Universidad Nacional Autónoma de México (National Autonomous University of Mexico)

Introduction

The International Division of Humanity

In October 1944, amid a flurry of intense lobbying efforts leading to the signing of the United Nations Charter in San Francisco, Dr. W. E. B. Du Bois received a letter from Judge Joseph Proskauer of the American Jewish Committee asking the distinguished scholar to sign on to the committee's draft of a "Declaration of Human Rights." "On the eve of liberation," Proskauer wrote, "we feel a particular urgency for all men of peace and goodwill to emphasize and reaffirm the godly concept of the dignity of the individual man." The judge ended the letter by writing that "we trust that you will join with us in presenting the Declaration of Human Rights to the American public. To this end, please sign and return one copy in the enclosed self-addressed envelope."[1] Prior to the receipt of this appeal, Du Bois had vociferously denounced the persecution of Jewish people in Europe in a number of essays, describing the genocide as the "supertragedy" of European civilization. In his response to Proskauer a couple of weeks later, however, he wrote the following:

> My Dear Sir, I have received your declaration of human rights and want to say frankly that I am greatly disappointed.... You say under paragraph two of your creed: "No plea of sovereignty shall ever again be allowed to permit any nation to deprive those within its borders of these fundamental rights on the claim that these matters are of internal concern." How about depriving people outside the borders of a country of their rights?... Under paragraph five you appeal for sympathy for persons driven from the land of their birth; but how about American Negroes, Africans, and Indians who have not been driven from their land of birth but are nonetheless deprived of their rights? Under paragraph six you want redress for those who wander the earth but how about those who do not wander and nevertheless are deprived of their fundamental human rights?... In other words,

> this declaration of rights has apparently no thought of the rights
> of Negroes, Indians, and South Sea Islanders. Why then call it the
> Declaration of Human Rights?[2]

In this Declaration's summary bypass of a range of historic and contemporary conditions of violence, Du Bois recognized a looming
danger: the new universal human was remarkably similar to previous ideological iterations of the Rights of Man. Indeed this was
neither the first nor the last time that Du Bois would object to a
postwar rearticulation of rights for reproducing an already existing
international division of humanity. A few months later in February
1945, Du Bois expressed a related set of concerns about the plans for
a "new" world government organization floated by the influential
Commission to Study the Organization of Peace. In response to their
proposal for "regional commissions" to oversee the "dependent territories" occupied by Axis powers, Du Bois wrote to the executive
director Clark Eichelberger that the commission's document "com-
bine[d] the interest in colonial peoples with the interest in imperial
objects and is too strongly weighted on the side of imperialism."[3]

Against these midcentury elisions of the color line, Du Bois submitted a proposal to the UN Conference stating that the "first
statute of international law" should read: "The colonial system of
government, however deeply rooted in history and custom, is today
undemocratic, socially dangerous and a main cause of wars [and] at
the earliest practical moment no nation or group shall be deprived
of effective voice in its own government and enjoyment of the four
freedoms."[4] His language never made it to the floor for consideration. Several years after his failed efforts to have "the rights of
dependent peoples to govern themselves" acknowledged in the UN
Charter, Du Bois served as one of the authors of the Civil Rights
Congress's 1951 petition to the UN in which the U.S. government,
the self-proclaimed world leader of human rights, was itself charged
with the crime of genocide.[5] Predictably, the UN did not respond.

Du Bois's efforts to speak on behalf of, in his words, "the
unrepresented 750,000,000" ran up against a formidable imperialist consensus determined to maintain a divided world. But despite
the *official* rejection of his appeals for a more critical reckoning
with imperial violence from 1492 onward, unofficial and popular
demands for a truly new international order have never subsided.
This book is intended to take its place alongside those rejected historical accounts that have long recognized that imperialist interests

and international justice can never be reconciled and to align with the long genealogy of collective movements organized to advance a genuinely new "internationalism of peoples."[6]

A Global Ethic?

The political utility of international human rights practice is a critical question for our time. Can human rights provide any protection from the vagaries of imperial violence? Can human rights serve to advance progressive politics in the contemporary world? Can human rights help to erase the lines of division that have long distinguished the human from the nonhuman? The intellectual left (communist, socialist, liberal, social democratic, anarchist) has been weighing in on this question with increasing frequency and urgency. The range of disagreement is pronounced. On one hand, human rights are seen as an answer to the search for an oppositional framework capable of contesting the globalized force and world devastations of contemporary capitalism.[7] In these scenarios, contemporary globalization is understood as having created new, objective conditions for progressive, even radical, opportunities that confer to "rights practice" an unprecedented power and imbue it with heavy doses of hope.[8] Against these optimistic formulations, on the other hand, human rights are believed to provide a convenient cover for the extension of capitalist–democratic uneven relations of power by reinforcing imperialist hegemonic control. In these scenarios, human rights are not a sign of hope, but part of an ominous trend toward the extension of a neoliberal, global capitalist hegemony.[9] In sum, the question of the politics of human rights in the contemporary period has generated theoretical debates that are wildly divergent in their assessment of the value of human rights.[10]

The proliferation of analyses on human rights derives both necessity and urgency from the contemporary ascendancy of rights as the privileged discourse for the symbolic articulation of international justice in an era of advanced globalized capitalism. The centering of human rights as the privileged mediational frame for international politics may now be said to mark a place of importance that exceeds even that of prior momentous conjunctures, such as in 1789 and 1848, when "the rights of man and the citizen" served as the ideational signifier for a critical refashioning of the bourgeois–imperial world. Indeed, human rights have increasingly come to define "the political" in this age of advanced capitalist globalization.

Human rights emerged as a key concept in the discourse of the postwar international with the passage of the Universal Declaration of Human Rights (adopted December 10, 1948). No other singular text has done more to shape the contours of the contemporary discourse on human rights. The Universal Declaration set forth an impressive array of human rights that all persons would receive "without distinction of any kind, such as race, colour, sex, language, religion, political or other opinion, national or social origin, property, birth or other status."[11] In the 1970s human rights became an increasingly favored tool through which activists in the global north sought to expose and mitigate a variety of extreme "abuses" to which individuals and groups around the world were subject (especially those that took place in formerly colonized territories). It was after the fall of the Berlin Wall and the end of real socialism, however, that human rights began to flourish as an international ethic.

Despite the commitment to advancing a new universality, however, we confront a grim postwar reality in which "never before, in absolute figures, never have so many men, women, and children been subjugated, starved, or exterminated on the earth."[12] As the late French philosopher Jacques Derrida aptly put it, it is in the face of this mounting crisis that a "new international" is being sought, one that:

> already denounces the limits of a discourse on human rights that will remain inadequate, sometimes hypocritical, and in any case formalistic and inconsistent with itself as long as the law of the market, the "foreign debt," the inequality of techno-scientific, military, and economic development maintain an effective inequality as monstrous as that which prevails today, to a greater extent than ever in the history of humanity.[13]

Given the dogged persistence of an international division of humanity grounded in the capitalist reproduction of "monstrous" economic disparities, it would seem that we need to reinvigorate our commitment to what radical communitarians around the planet — whether adherents of leveling, communism, anarchism, or "traditional" communal practice — have long advanced as the means to living as humans. At the same time, in our increasingly interconnected world, we also need a radically different understanding of the ideological relation between the human and the nonhuman and the role that international institutions and discourses play in maintaining and regulating the differential orders of humanity. For this broad politico-philosophical project we must find new ways of reckoning with the heterogeneous violences of the past and present for a different kind of human future, as necessary as it is elusive.

Rebellious Specters from Communism to Decolonization

There is, then, a growing recognition (including among human rights advocates) that the dominant models of human rights practice are more or less incapable of accounting for, let alone responding to, the increasing capacities for cruelty and the proliferating forms of violence in our contemporary world. Given this, it would seem that we need some means of advancing a new episteme of political violence, one that affords us better ways through which to recognize and map acts and conditions of violence and, we hope, to develop more effective means and strategies through which to confront and contest the global fields of brutality. To these ends, it is useful to reengage the history of postwar human rights praxis and to examine in a more critical fashion what other ways of knowing and responding to violence have been used and developed, concurrent with those of human rights, yet largely out of view and grossly underappreciated. For this project, we would do well to consider what other epistemic forms and political practices have attended to this history of postwar human rights as that which had to be negated and refused in order for the liberal model of rights to emerge as the privileged ideological frame through which excessive cruelty was conceived and interpreted.

In their famous opening to the *Manifesto of the Communist Party* (1848), Marx and Engels announced the presence of a specter that was "haunting Europe — the specter of Communism." Against this specter, "all the powers of old Europe [had] entered into a holy alliance . . . Pope and Czar, Metternich and Guiznot, French Radicals and German police-spies."[14] A century later, as representatives of the United Nations General Assembly gathered together to ratify the Universal Declaration of Human Rights, a new set of collective specters had made their appearance in the world.[15] Like the earlier historic conjuncture, this twentieth-century holy alliance confronted a "many-headed hydra" whose sheer multiplicity of forms and features compelled an imperialist unification of unprecedented scope.[16]

On the one hand, the specter of barbarism *in Europe* served as the most present of apparitions. As numerous historians have noted, without the Nazi Holocaust, there is no Universal Declaration.[17] But while the absolute brutality of the mass industrial killing of Jewish people served as the occasion and wellspring for the great performative event known as the *Declaration*, other specters were conspicuously present, even if less recognized.[18] The haunting presence of these other specters registers, however dimly, in the preamble to the UDHR: "Whereas it is essential, if a man is not to be compelled to have recourse, as a last resort, to rebellion against tyranny and oppression, that human rights should be protected by the rule of law." What was this curious figure of "rebellion against tyranny and oppression" against which human rights "should be protected" and in relation to which it derives its raison d'être? After all, the barbarity of Nazism was not, strictly speaking, a rebellious affair. And yet here, by way of opening onto the performative space of the UDHR, the sign of this other spectral force is compelled to emerge as that which must, in the last instance, be warded off. What was this unnamed and unmarked haunting figure against which the new alliance of global powers had come to develop and assert the new weapon of international human rights?

There was, in fact, quite a vertiginous array of alternative forms of universality present at the moment of the inception of the UDHR. Counter and contrary to the lofty, abstract juridical ideals of international human rights, such alternative conceptions and practices of freedom were much more directly rooted in the actualities of struggle. In relatively short order we would have innumerable signs of their veritable presence under the heading of national independence: India (1947), Indonesia (1950), Egypt (1952), Vietnam (1954/1975), Ghana (1957), Algeria (1962), and Kenya (1963), to name but a few. They would also appear in the name of revolution: China (1949), Cuba (1959), Nicaragua (1979), and Iran (1979). And, lastly, they appeared in various international assemblies gathered to discuss the futures of freedom: the Fifth Pan-African Congress (1945), Bandung (1955), and the Tricontinental Congress of the Peoples of Asia, Africa, and Latin America (Havana 1966) again, to name but a few. Across continents and across the world the irrepressible dynamic of decolonization surged, giving ample ex post facto evidence that this was in fact the "rebellious specter" that the Universal Declaration sought to keep at bay.[19]

Imperialist Law

Since 1945 the advance of global capitalism has been, in the main, driven by the ascendance of U.S. imperial power (economic and military). According to the political economist Samir Amin, the reconfiguration of global power from the Second World War up to the end of the Cold War was "characterized by the emergence of a collective imperialism" involving the "triad" of the United States, Europe (west of the Polish frontier), and Japan.[20] It is in this context of accelerated, militarized global capitalism that the postwar dynamic of decolonization throughout Asia and Africa and the struggles for socialism (both inside and outside the West) must be understood. Of particular importance in this regard are the aggressive disarticulations between the twin dynamics of decolonization and socialist revolution, commonly misread as their historic failure, as effected through the global triumph of capitalist imperialism. As critical theorist Aijaz Ahmad puts it in his sweeping outline of the "contradictory unity of the world in our epoch":

> the consolidation and postwar expansion in all the homelands of advanced capital, reflected as much in the imperialist military machine as in the globalized corporate economy, meant that throughout this period capital was to command enormous power to condemn every country which even attempted to introduce socialism to a perpetual war economy under conditions of acute scarcity and low levels of social development.... Every one of these states became, in the very moment of inception and for many years thereafter, a national-security state — always with a high degree of regimentation, frequently sequestered and pauperized as well.[21]

With actually existing socialism in retreat and competing capitals on the rise, the United States moved to impose its leadership over the triad (and its various neocolonial incorporations) through military control of the planet. A central tenet behind this hegemonic maneuvering is that the "sovereign national interests of the United States" should hold sway over the entire international field of legitimate political behavior (including arrogating to itself the right to wage "preventative wars"). This "new" global military strategy of the United States, inaugurated with the bombings of Hiroshima and Nagasaki, now serves as the primary means to ensure privileged access to all of the world's natural resources. And while the durability of such a strategy is very much in doubt, the intent is clear: "military control of the planet is the means to impose, as a last resort, the draining of 'tribute' through political violence — as a substitute for the 'spontaneous' flow of capital that offsets the American deficit, the Achilles heel of U.S. hegemony."[22]

It is precisely here, in a post–Cold War context marked by an unprecedented militarization of the world by a singular hegemonic power, that human rights emerged as the privileged epistemic form for political violence. This does not, in itself, guarantee the alignment of human rights with imperialist power or hegemonic institutions, but it does carry profound implications for the future of international legal instruments of all kinds. In order to gain an adequate account of what U.S. monopolistic military power means for international law, we have to shift our analytical perspective from one that assumes that imperialism is a problem *for* international law, to one that grasps their mutually constitutive relationship. This is one of the critical interventions of China Miéville's recent Marxist analysis of international law wherein he argues that the dynamic structure and form of international law "*assumes* imperialism."[23] Thus more important than any historic inscription of international law within European culture or dependency on Eurocentric concepts, we have to understand how international institutions operate within the structures of imperialist power. This is most evident, as Derrida has pointed out, in the disjuncture between decision making and enforcement:

> This supposedly universal international law remains, in its application, largely dominated by particular nation-States. Almost always their technoeconomic and military power prepares and applies, in other words, *carries* the decision. . . . Countless examples, recent or not so recent, would amply demonstrate this, whether it is a question of deliberations and resolutions of the United Nations or of putting into practice or the "enforcement" of these decisions: the incoherence, discontinuity, inequality of States before the law, the hegemony of certain States over military power in the service of international law, this is what, year after year, day after day, we are forced to acknowledge.[24]

Unfortunately, as I demonstrate throughout this book, the ascendancy of human rights as the privileged frame through which the relation between political violence and international law is conceived works to occlude just such a critical acknowledgment.

Human Rights versus Decolonization

This book is organized around the oppositional relation between two major postwar political forms, human rights and decolonization. Setting these critical practices in relation to one another has the twofold effect of bringing into relief the ways in which the contemporary human rights regime obscures the dialectic between (imperial) violence and (international) law and of demonstrating what kinds of understanding become possible and necessary when force and law are conceived as operating in a symbiotic fashion. In the opening chapters I examine two geopolitical encounters separated by three decades in which human rights organizations from the global north and anticolonial movements from the global south advanced decidedly divergent political programs in response to conditions of state terror. In each context, albeit in highly variable and geographically and historically specific ways, this divergence worked against the building of any effective networks of affinity and solidarity across the international divisions of humanity. In this way the first two chapters offer critical rejoinders to the glib talk of transnational NGO advocacy networks and global civil society that abound in the anthropological and social scientific discourses of today.[25]

Chapter 1 opens with an analysis of Amnesty International's 1964 *disqualification* of South African Nelson Mandela as a prisoner of conscience. Despite having initially adopted Mandela as a victim of human rights abuse, the nascent international NGO quickly voted to drop the antiapartheid activist following his trial statement. In his statement from the dock, Mandela defended the African National Congress's use of organized political violence as a necessary (and ethical) response in the struggle against the racist South African state. Mandela's highly nuanced argument in favor of the selective and limited use of counterviolence was born out of the historic failures evident in the fact that more than fifty years of nonviolent struggle had been consistently met with greater and greater levels of state violence and repression. The long-running inability of the resistance organization to wrest even modest concessions from the white minority government through more generally sanctioned uses of force (petitions for enfranchisement, appeals for the recognition of rights, demands for better living and working conditions, organizing of strikes, etc.) left black South Africans with but one option: armed struggle. In Mandela's own account, examined in detail in the opening chapter, by the early 1960s South Africa was on the cusp of a full-scale civil war in which ANC supporters "were developing disturbing ideas of terrorism."[26] For the responsible political organization there was no longer a choice, strategic or ethical, to be made between violence or nonviolence, and so the ANC maneuvered to organize and direct the proliferation of violence in a disciplined and effective manner. Neither the apartheid state nor the international human rights organization, however, accepted Mandela's argument as he was sentenced to life imprisonment and removed from Amnesty's worldwide list of prisoners of conscience.

Mandela's disqualification is little more than a historic footnote in the annals of human rights practice, variably conscripted as part of Amnesty's longstanding, absolute commitment to the principle of nonviolence or actively forgotten now that the anticolonial, communist guerrilla (Mandela) has been resurrected in the post–Apartheid era as a paradigmatic symbol of the success of international human rights. Against these revisionist confabulations, I read the case of Mandela's disqualification as a world-historic encounter between two forms of postwar international political practice, decolonization and nongovernmental human rights, whose historical and political epistemologies are demonstrably and starkly at odds with one another. In this frame, Amnesty's decision serves as a pivotal moment in the contemporary formation of international human rights activism insofar as it materially activates the *anti*-anticolonial logic implicit in the Universal Declaration through its de facto alignment with the (Apartheid) state and its (juridical) monopoly over the definition and terms of "acceptable" and "legitimate" uses of force. Rather than being a minor incident of little significance, the disqualification of Mandela marks the point at which the postwar discourse of human rights, as advanced by the major international NGO, becomes a default ally of state violence by rejecting out-of-hand any and all claims to the right of armed resistance regardless of conditions, past or present.

Chapter 2 takes up the question of how the foundational oppositionality between decolonizing praxis and human rights has been reconfigured since the early 1960s, as one formerly colonized nation after another gained independence and as more and more political collectivities on both sides of the international divide began to deploy the discourse of human rights. Out of this geopolitical

reformation, "new" and "old" collectivities have emerged to contest lines of force within and between the North and South, and
this chapter examines two such recent social movements: the International Lesbian and Gay Human Rights Commission (ILGHRC)
and the indigenous army of the EZLN (the "Zapatistas"). In this
encounter I examine the solidarity work from the global gay north
as advanced by ILGHRC around a series of murders of working-
class transgenders in Chiapas, Mexico, between 1991 and 1993
and the murders of five affluent gay men in Mexico City over the
course of a week in 1992. In this particular instance, the collective
travesti murders carried out by state agents (the police with possible
involvement of the army) were initially met with expressions of sympathy by ILGHRC but no action. This would change in July 1992,
however, after the (unrelated) murder of Doctor Francisco Estrada
in Mexico City. In contrast to the killing of "gender-aberrant,"
working-class *travestis* in Tuxtla Gutiérrez (Chiapas), the murder
of Dr. Estrada generated an immediate and vigorous response from
gay activists to the North as he had formed the first AIDS organization in Mexico and was well known in bourgeois cosmopolitan gay
circles. Along with urgent calls for an investigation into the Estrada
murder, the *travesti* assassinations in Chiapas suddenly appeared in
the press reports released by ILGHRC as a supplement to claims of
rampant "homophobia" throughout Mexico.

This institutional case study reveals under what terms and conditions subjects become legible within the emergent discourse of
global gay rights and how a recognizably older set of international
divisions (geopolitical, racial, class, gender) continue to operate
through the new demands for sexual recognition. The ostensibly
"progressive" challenge that ILGHRC promotes in relation to the
patriarchal and heterosexist universalism of the Enlightenment is
shown to be contravened by the "gay international's" inscription
within a neoimperial, modern episteme all-too-ready to sanction the
exclusionary interests of metropolitan sexual identity politics and
advance a universalist, bourgeois cosmopolitanism.[27] In contrast to
the market-driven, transnational solidarities advanced through the
neoimperialist internationalism of the "Gay International," different modes of struggle for sexual recognition and political solidarity
have been circulating across Mexico and the Americas that take
their cues from liberatory practices forged out of long histories of
anticolonial struggle. And so chapter 2 closes with a consideration
of at least one way in which transgender activists and peasant rebels

(among many others) have recently come together in the forging of critical communities of affinity. In 2006, some twelve years after successfully seizing and defending autonomous zones within the state of Chiapas, the Zapatistas embarked on a tour of Mexico, dubbed "la Otra Campaña." In their attempt to construct another way of practicing politics, the indigenous rebels sought to open a dialogic space for a new kind of national network and in the process lay the groundwork for a new model for international solidarity. In contrast to identity-structured, rights-based models of political practice, this emergent collectivity is not bound by universal belonging to a particular category (gay, indigenous, women, or even the human) but by ideological affinity ("from below and to the left") and an absolute refusal to accept any modified project of modernity that reproduces the colonial capitalist divisions of humanity. The "Other Campaign," then, provides yet another sign that decolonization is a dynamic series of processes and projects whose ends are not in gaining national independence (although that remains vitally necessary and far from realized), but in nothing less than the building of a new internationalism, long-in-the-making but with considerable solidarity work to be done.

While the first two chapters focus on the material practice of select postwar struggles in order to demonstrate the divergent politics between decolonization and human rights, subsequent chapters consider how the ideology of human rights has come to play an increasingly critical role in the legitimation of contemporary imperialist interventions. The rearticulation of the terms of "international intervention" after the Cold War (just wars, preemptive invasions, humanitarian operations, etc.) relies on "new" frameworks of legitimacy for which the communications industries generally, and human rights discourse in particular, have proven indispensable.[28] As Michael Hardt and Antonio Negri argue in their account of contemporary imperialism, "the Empire's powers of intervention might be best understood as beginning not directly with its weapons of lethal force but rather with its moral instruments" of which the most important forces are those "global, regional, and local organizations that are dedicated to relief work and the protection of human rights."[29] Building on this claim, my account of the spread of human rights across "the immaterial nexuses of the production of language, communication, and the symbolic" is shown to result from its ideological capacity to produce subjects and subjectivities consistent with the self-validating structures of imperialist power. The symbiotic relationship between contemporary human rights and imperialism is most evident in the representation of, and intervention in, "ethnic conflicts" insofar as such antagonisms are presumed to provide the sharpest contrast between the colonial past and the cosmopolitan future. Chapter 3 examines the increasingly prolific transit between the ideology of human rights, the communication industries, and imperialist structures of legitimacy through an analysis of two recent films, Terry George's *Hotel Rwanda* (2004) and Michael Haneke's *Caché* (2005).

In the cinematic representation of the Rwandan genocide, George's *Hotel Rwanda* stages the catastrophic events of April 1994 through the relationship between the local hotel manager, Paul Rusesabagina, and the United Nations peacekeeper, Colonel Oliver. Rusesabagina is figured as the heroic protagonist who deserves rescue but does not receive it, while Colonel Oliver is cast as the well-meaning but frustrated official who bears the weight of shame brought about through the failure of international institutions to intercede on behalf of the Rwandan people. In its near-exclusive focus on these two figures, *Hotel Rwanda* enfolds the complex histories and materialities of genocidal violence into a moral tale to be popularly consumed as the "lesson of Rwanda." The lesson has two critical vectors, one directed toward the past of Rwanda, *we should have intervened*, and another directed toward any future genocide, *we can never let this happen again*. In the former modality, any actual record of Western involvement (before, during, and after the genocide) is erased in favor of figuring the West as an exterior agent to events in Rwanda. In the latter, any question of the desirability of such intervention is elided in the generalized promotion of the West as humanitarian savior.

In contrast to *Hotel Rwanda,* Michael Haneke's *Caché* (2005) uses the 1961 slaughter of some two hundred Algerian protestors by the Paris police as the basis for a fictional tale about the colonial return of the repressed in the life of Georges Laurent. Haneke deploys a mystery format to force the bourgeois protagonist to reckon with his own personal involvement in the history of French colonial violence against the Algerian people. In this postmodernist exposing of the shame of the West, Haneke deftly makes the psycho-affective machinations of colonial disavowal visible as Georges stubbornly refuses to acknowledge any responsibility, past or present, for the violent consequences of his actions. Georges's bad conscience is set off against the benign passivity of the Algerian immigrant Majid, whose childhood victimization is brought to a tragic close some forty odd years later with his act of suicide in Georges's presence. After the death of the colonial other, Majid's son continues to disturb Georges's desire to be free of the past, while seeming to conspire with Georges's son, Pierrot, in the making of a postcolonial future yet to come.

In a putative advance over the Orientalist imaginary of imperial cinema, both *Hotel Rwanda* and *Caché* stage the ethical superiority of the third world subject over and against the shameful actions of the West. But while this redistribution of ethical evaluation appears as symbolic reparation for the historic wrongs of the colonial past, the "new" field of rights and responsibilities rearticulates the older lines of colonial division through a differential economy of obligation. On one side of the divide, the formerly colonized subject is obligated to passively accept the cosmopolitan norms of civility in exchange for the recognition of their humanity. Given this set of obligations, it is not surprising that Paul (*Hotel Rwanda*) and Majid (*Caché*) are figured as exemplary models of domesticated postcolonial otherness, demanding nothing and dutifully accepting their subordinate place in the structures of capitalist globalization. On the other side, the rights and responsibilities for the Western subject are tied to the very derivation and enforcement of cosmopolitan norms. In their failure to adequately perform these tasks, Georges Laurent (*Caché*) and Colonel Oliver (*Hotel Rwanda*) subject the West to charges of shame within the courts of public opinion. In the symbolic production of this nonreciprocal economy of duties, the liberal cinematic imagination supplies the ideological structure of imperialist intervention with models of subjectivity integral to the legitimation of future deployments of humanitarian force.

In the wake of deadly catastrophes like genocide, apartheid, and dictatorship, an increasing number of states have turned to the "Truth Commission" as an institutionalized means of postviolence redress. As the crowning achievement of late twentieth-century human rights practice, the Truth Commission is commonly conceived as a recording apparatus that works against historical amnesia/disavowal by means of a therapeutic, collective recounting of state terror. As an ethico-political form with a unique relation to the historical and the literary (in its archival mode and its reliance on the *testimonio*), the Truth Commission is designed to convert the violence of the past into the nonviolence of the future. Chapter 4 looks at two literary narratives, Ariel Dorfman's play *Death and the Maiden* (1991) and Claribel Alegría and Darwin Flakoll's chronicle *Death of Somoza* (1993), in terms of how each offers a critical account of the politics of the Truth Commission form.

In Dorfman's play, written after the end of Pinochet's dictatorial rule in Chile, a woman (Paulina) reencounters a man (Dr. Miranda) who raped and tortured her in the aftermath of the 1973 coup d'etat. Paulina's husband, Gerardo, a human rights lawyer, has been appointed to the State Commission to investigate the crimes of the dictatorship. With this triad, Dorfman staged the "difficult transition to democracy" through the irreducible tensions between private justice (revenge) and national reconciliation (consensus). While the prospect of documenting the truth of what happened animates Gerardo's faith in preventing future violence, Paulina senses that her desires for justice will be betrayed under the restricted purview of the commission. In the last dramatic instance, her right of revenge is sacrificed to the dictates of a consensual model of democratic stability.

In contrast to the tensions played out in Dorfman's text, Claribel Alegría and Darwin Flakoll's *Death of Somoza* (1993) chronicles the actions of a small group of Argentinian commandos as they carry out a successful mission to assassinate the deposed Nicaraguan dictator, Anastasio Somoza Debayle. Based on interviews with the seven survivors of the act of "tyrannicide," Alegría and Flakoll narratively reconstruct the events leading up to and following the 1980 assassination.[30] In this account the dramatic tension is not provided by any ethical deliberations (as in "Should they kill him?" "Do they have the right to kill him?" etc.) but rather by the question of "how are they going to pull it off?" In their refusal to recast the act of tyrannicide as a (primarily) moral question, the authors allow for the emergence of an alternative conception and practice of politics and solidarity: a popular politics of counterviolence.

In my analysis, both texts, in highly divergent ways, afford us an opportunity to engage the question of the (non)convertibility of violence into nonviolence in ways otherwise occluded by a human rights politic with its abstract idealization of nonviolence.[31] As Étienne Balibar has argued, "extreme violence arises from institutions as much as it arises against them, and it is not possible to escape this circle by 'absolute' decisions such as choosing between a violent or a nonviolent politics, or between force and law." Consequently, he suggests, "the only 'way' out of this circle is to invent a politics of violence, or to introduce the issue of violence . . . into the concept and practice of politics."[32] Against the therapeutic design of the Truth Commission form, the literary recounting of collective justice in these critical texts reworks the politics of the *testimonio* as a counterarchive of struggle that refuses the demands of reconciliation in exchange for representational agency.[33] Where Dorfman's text ultimately pulls back from "advocating" the use of violence as a legitimate response to state terror (but not before unleashing this "other scene of politics"), Alegría and Flakoll's recounting of tyrannicide challenges the principle of nonviolence as it has been advanced over the past half century by human rights activists on both sides of the international division of humanity.

In contrast to strategies of civility that take nonviolence as their axiomatic principle, international law as their means, and global civil society as their ends, postwar decolonizing praxis has insistently sought a renewal of the idea of revolution grounded in the recognition that violence is the sine qua non of imperialism. In this alternative frame, the globalized structures and structuring of violence serve as the foundation out of which any politics of liberation must be forged. As a way into this other strategy of reckoning with contemporary conditions of imperialist globalization, chapter 5 revisits the unique theorization of "violence" that Frantz Fanon articulated in his infamous last book, *The Wretched of the Earth* (1961). In Fanon's conception, the totalizing nature of colonial violence must not only be challenged by the absolute violence of decolonization, but such a confrontation also carries with it a political obligation to take sides. Subsequent intellectual analyses of Fanon's work from Hannah Arendt to Homi Bhabha have been, however, largely unable and unwilling to countenance his injunction to affirm the material praxis of anticolonial violence — thereby blunting the critical force of a decolonizing approach in which politics and violence are conceived as inseparable. Instead the postcolonial partitioning of Fanon into early (psychoanalytic) and late (revolutionary) phases has served as a means to avoid the paradox of his advocacy for using the very same *technē* that defines the form and field of relationality in the colonies: violence. In order to adequately grasp the real alternative that decolonizing theory poses to liberal humanism and Western imperialism, this "contradictory" praxis must be engaged.

In his strategic advocacy of (anticolonial) violence as a response to (colonial) violence and nationalist consciousness as the only means to internationalism, Fanon was well aware that every means available in the struggle for decolonization was potentially subject to counterhistories both during the fight for and after the gaining of national independence. In this way Fanon offered, well beyond what was specific to the conditions of colonialism proper (and wholly relevant for today), a critical set of political directives developed out of the relative certainty that any strategic appropriation of dominant structures and forms in the course of struggle must reckon with the corrupted histories of those same forms after the achievement of their tactical ends.[34] This enduring lesson should trouble, albeit in different ways, any nondialectical advocacy of either human rights or decolonization, insofar as any readily available "way" out of structures of domination is, both likely and at the same time, a "way" back in. In the case of human rights, for example, inserting the formal equality of the universal human into structures of violence regulated by domestic *and* international law subjects any "successful" appropriation of juridical terms to swift and effective counterappropriation.[35] As a dialectical theory of decolonizing violence and imperialist counterappropriation (the neocolonial), Fanon's work serves as a critical foundation for any anti-imperialist analytic circumspect about the reformability of international law and the potential pitfalls of rearticulating dominant forms in a pseudo-revolutionary modality.

In recent years a select number of theorists have taken up this Fanonian analytic (if not in name, at least in form) in the production of contemporary critiques of international institutions and cosmopolitan discourses, including those of international law (Miéville), the United Nations (Danilo Zolo), international human rights (Pheng Cheah), and transnational solidarity (M. Jacqui Alexander).[36] What distinguishes this emergent body of critical scholarship is the recognition that the postwar re-formation of international institutions did not constitute a break with the historical structures of colonial violence but instead was part and parcel of an imperialist-directed reorganization of relations within and between contemporary state and social formations: the colonial, the neocolonial, and the neoimperial.[37] Consequently, each critique advances an anticosmopolitan theory of political practice on the grounds that the new humanism of globalization has an intimate relation to the internationalized economy of corporate–capitalist warfare and development (whether carried forth under the banner of neoliberalism, socialism, communism, or some other form of neodevelopmentalism). While the dominant tendencies within the fields of international relations and political science assume that some form of supranational, juridical institution is indispensable to the realization of the ideals of world peace and human justice, anti-imperialist theorizations direct us to look *outside the law* for sources of revolutionary, international transformation. In this decolonizing register, the displacement of the juridical makes possible a critical reckoning oriented toward the building of local, national, regional, and international movements in a counter-counterrevolutionary mode. In other words, it is only through the effective neutralization of imperialist power, with its enormous capacity for counterrevolutionary and counterinsurrectional violence, that any genuinely new international becomes possible. Here the emergent anti-imperialist analytics of contemporary decolonizing theory align with the principles expressed in "The Bamako Appeal," as articulated at the 2006 World Social Forum:

> The solidarity of all peoples, North and South, in the construction of a universal civilization can not be based on the notion that, since everyone lives on the same planet, it should be possible to neglect the conflicts of interest between the different classes and nations that make up the real world. Such solidarity requires going beyond the laws and values of capitalism and the imperialism that is inherent to it.... Fifty years after the Bandung Conference, the Bamako Appeal calls for a Bandung of the peoples of the South, those who are the victims of the expansion of really existing capitalism, and calls for a reconstruction of a peoples' front of the South that is capable of defeating the imperialism of the dominant economic powers and the military hegemony of the United States. This anti-imperialist front would not oppose the peoples of the South to those of the North. On the contrary, it is a foundation for the construction of a global internationalism that involves everyone in the building of a common civilization in its diversity.[38]

Toward a Nonjuridical Reckoning

The palpable excitement from liberal quarters that the world was on the brink of a truly new international order following the fall of the Berlin Wall has subsided considerably in the wake of post–Cold War catastrophes from Rwanda to Darfur, Bosnia to Afghanistan, and Abu Ghraib to Guantánamo, as well as from the specter of a permanent world war to come, the "war on terror." In one of an ongoing

series of tests of the strength of the postwar international apparatus to advance global peace, the world's attention was recently (and
once again) drawn to the region where the international division of
humanity appears in its most stark and intransigent form. In January 2009, after more than a week of aerial bombardments, Israeli
ground troops moved into the Gaza Strip and for two weeks laid
siege to its isolated and sequestered inhabitants. By the end of this
particular, and particularly brutal, twenty-one-day assault on the
largest open-air prison in the world, thirteen hundred Palestinians
had been murdered.

In the midst of the attack, the U.S. Congress quickly moved
to pass a resolution declaring its unwavering support for Israel's
actions. The new U.S. president (Obama) adopted the same position
as the outgoing president (Bush), albeit with slightly more rhetorical
eloquence. The United Nations issued a series of pronouncements
condemning the invasion but was unable to advance any cease-fire
declarations or war crimes investigations as the United States stood
by, prepared and able to block any international resolutions. The
only international institution apparently willing and (potentially)
able to take up the case of war crimes committed by the Israeli
government was the International Criminal Court (ICC). However, even these postslaughter, juridical deliberations were bogged
down by whether the claimant in the case, the Palestinian Authority,
was "enough like a state" to bring charges before the court.[39] Of
course such a determination will carry little consequence as Israel,
like the United States, is not a full-fledged member of the ICC
and is under no legal obligation to send Israeli troops, comman-
ders, or political officials to any trial conducted at The Hague.[40]
Quite instructively, Hamas, the democratically elected representatives of the people of Gaza and the putative target of the Israeli
assault, is not likely to bother trying to bring charges before any
international institution, having long since recognized that international court rulings carry no force for powerful states. As one
Hamas spokesperson put it after a "favorable" International Court
of Justice ruling in 2004 against the "West Bank wall" erected by
the Israeli government: "What is the point in fighting legal battles
when Israel and the U.S. are so ready to reject court rulings they do
not like?"[41]

In its own defense, the Zionist-controlled Israeli government
declares that it has not broken any international laws: "We have
international lawyers at every level of command whose job it

is to authorize targeting decisions, rules of engagement.... We don't think we have breached international law in any of these instances."[42] While this claim may strike liberal international legal scholars and humanist laypersons as, at best, disingenuous and, at worst, morally reprehensible, it is not entirely implausible. Much of the current slaughter, this or that excess withstanding, may well be perfectly legal. And it is this fact that Western critics of this action, as well as critics of the ongoing U.S. wars in Iraq and Afghanistan, have consistently failed to grasp and theorize.[43] In other words, rather than simply assuming that the inhuman slaughter of persons on a mass scale must be or is necessarily "against the law," what if we suppose that international law is, at best, neutral or completely ineffectual on such matters and, at worst, fully complicit and legitimating?

This is not just a hypothetical exercise, as China Miéville has recently demonstrated, but rather is consistent with the actual historical record of international law and imperialist violence from their origins on into the twenty-first century.[44] If we leave aside for a moment our erstwhile longings for a harmonious future for humankind, what this suggests is that part of what has occluded our ability to reckon with the past is the superordinate investment we have made with the promise of a juridical future.[45] In this sense it is not just a more exhaustive reckoning with the past and present of imperialist violence that is needed but, more specifically, a *nonjuridical reckoning*. For this, our starting point should be neither the law nor any desire for a "progressive" appropriation of the law, but the mounting dead for whom the law was either a useless means of defense or an accomplice to their murder.[46]

Conscience Denied

Amnesty International and
the Antirevolution of the 1960s

On May 28, 1961, a small group of British lawyers, writers, and publishers, headed by Peter Benenson, launched a public campaign for the release of eight prisoners from around the world. The campaign began with the article "The Forgotten Prisoners" published in the *Observer* (England) and picked up the following day by *Le Monde* (France), the *New York Herald Tribune* (United States), *Die Welt* (Germany), *Journal de Genève* (Switzerland), *Berlingske Tidende* (Denmark), and *Politiken* (Sweden). In the notice, the authors announced the establishment of "an office in London to collect information about the names, numbers, and conditions of what we have decided to call 'Prisoners of Conscience.' "[1] This event now marks the birth of the most influential nongovernmental human rights organization of the twentieth century: Amnesty International (AI). It was also the international debut for the category of the prisoner of conscience (POC).

Both the emergence of a new organization, Amnesty International, and a new concept, the "prisoner of conscience," occupy important positions in post-1960 formations of nongovernmental modes of international political activism. AI is consistently reputed to be one of the most influential human rights organizations in the world, and this reputation has not faltered during its nearly fifty years of existence. While the proliferation of international, nongovernmental human rights organizations has certainly led to the development of competing models of human rights practice, Amnesty's methods remain the best known, the most studied, and the most frequently replicated. With currently more than 1.8 million members in more than 150 countries in every region of the world, its enduring success as an NGO is remarkable.[2]

The durability and inordinate influence of this organization affords us a privileged vantage point from which to examine the formative basis of NGO human rights activism in the postwar era. A close look at the historical context within which Amnesty emerged and the manner in which the founders wrestled with the relative misuse or nonuse of human rights from 1948 to 1960 tells us a great deal about how and why human rights has subsequently become a formidable discourse in the post–World War II construction of what Edward Said referred to as a "new universality":

> Constructing a "new universality" has preoccupied various international authorities since World War II. Milestones are of course the Universal Declaration of Human Rights, the Geneva Conventions, and an impressive battery of protocols for the treatment of refugees, minorities, prisoners, workers, children, students, and women. ... In addition, a wide range of nongovernmental national and international agencies like Amnesty, the Organization for Human Rights, and the Human Rights Watch committees monitor and publicize human rights abuses.[3]

It is neither insignificant nor incidental to Amnesty's success as an organization that its first political category of intervention was the "prisoner of conscience," a term that did not even appear in the 1948 Universal Declaration of Human Rights. Amnesty's early focus on the prisoner of conscience has only expanded over its history, with more than forty thousand prisoners of conscience having been adopted by the organization, and it continues to constitute the core of its operations despite the exceptional growth of the organization and the frequent refashioning of its mandate. The impressive legacy that Amnesty has built around this particular concept raises a number of critical questions: Why did Amnesty make the figure of the prisoner of conscience so central to the structure of its international human rights practice? Why did they articulate a new concept of political imprisonment at this historical juncture and in these terms? Why did Amnesty's founders surmise that individuals from around the world, or at least those in the wealthy North, would respond to the plight of "prisoners of conscience" regardless of their locations of confinement? Why did the whole complex of human rights coalesce around the figure of the "POC" such that it became "one of the most popularly used expressions in the human rights field"?[4] Does the deployment of this concept tells us something specific about the politics of international, nongovernmental human rights activism, or at least how the early activists viewed such a politic? And lastly, does the development and deployment of the concept of the prisoner of conscience enhance our understanding of how these early activists conceived of the politics of international (in)visibility and how to move beyond the Cold War contaminations that hitherto regulated which events, conditions, and subjects of violence became visible in an international frame?

In Defense of Violence

The new concept of the prisoner of conscience was defined as including "any person who is physically restrained (by imprisonment or otherwise) from expressing (in any form of words or symbols) any opinion which he honestly holds and which does not advocate or condone personal violence."[5] There are a number of significant qualifications in this initial formulation that serve to distinguish the POC from the older and much wider conception of the political prisoner.[6] The first notable limiting condition is that of "expression," whereby the prisoner of conscience is conceived as someone whose "speech" or "voice" is the mode of action for which they have been physically restrained. This limiting condition privileging the voice is further delimited by requiring that the content of the persecuted speech "not advocate or condone personal violence." Indeed something of the anecdotal prehistory of Amnesty International is said to have begun with a case of political persecution involving an expressive gesture. As the story goes, it was in 1960 that Benenson read a newspaper account about two Portuguese students imprisoned under the Salazar regime "for raising their glasses in public in a toast to freedom." Upon reading about this incident, Benenson decided to organize a letter-writing campaign to pressure for the release of the students.[7]

A few months later, in early 1961, Benenson and the initial group launched its now momentous "Appeal for Amnesty" on behalf of eight "forgotten prisoners":

> Agostino Neto, Angolan poet and later president, held without charge for nearly one year;

Constantin Noica, Romanian philosopher sentenced to twenty-five years imprisonment for conspiring against the security of the state and spreading propaganda hostile to the regime;

Antonio Amat, Spanish lawyer imprisoned for trying to form a coalition of democratic groups under Franco's rule, on trial since November of 1958;

Ashton Jones, U.S. minister repeatedly beaten and imprisoned in Louisiana and Texas for demanding equal rights for African Americans;

Patrick Duncan, white South African jailed for his opposition to apartheid, whose sentence included forbidding him from attending or addressing any meeting for five years;

Toni Ambatielos, Greek Communist and trade unionist;

Cardinal Mindszenty, Hungary, former prisoner and now political refugee;

Josef Beran, Archbishop of Prague, currently in custody.[8]

Modest success from this initial campaign on behalf of the "forgotten prisoners" (Beran, for instance, was released although he was banned from religious activities) generated the funds and interest necessary to build an organization devoted to the release of political prisoners worldwide. By the end of the year, there were Amnesty chapters throughout Western Europe as well as one in the United States.

In late 1964, however, the growing but still embryonic organization became embroiled in its first major internal controversy. The turmoil began when the question of the unconditional terms of the "nonviolence" clause appeared to necessitate the disqualification of a previously adopted prisoner of conscience: South African activist Nelson Mandela. Mandela had been unanimously conferred prisoner of conscience status in 1962. At that time, Mandela was in Pretoria Central Prison (South Africa) serving five years on charges of "incitement to strike" and "leaving the country without a valid permit."[9] As a strike organizer, fighting against the brutalities of the racist white South African regime, Mandela qualified as a subject worthy of human rights defense and received Amnesty's support. But in 1964, all of this changed when Mandela delivered a public statement before the court explaining why he and his fellow resistance fighters had decided to use violence to overthrow the racist South African state.

While still serving his initial sentence, Mandela was convicted along with eight other men from the African National Congress (ANC) on charges of "sabotage and conspiracy to overthrow the Government by revolution" and "by assisting an armed invasion of South Africa by foreign troops." Mandela's speech on April 20, 1964, opened the case for the defense. He did not plead his, or his co-conspirators, innocence: "some of the things so far told to the Court are true and some are untrue. I do not, however, deny that I planned sabotage." With the "admission of guilt" clearly made, Mandela's speech before the court became a historical treatise on the necessity for armed struggle in the contemporary context of the Republic of South Africa. Moreover, his account was a defense of the ethicality of using violence as a strategic method — and when, where, and under what conditions such strategic actions might be deemed both necessary and morally justifiable. As Mandela argued:

> ... the hard facts were that fifty years of non-violence had brought the African people nothing but more and more repressive legislation, and fewer and fewer rights. It may not be easy for this Court to understand, but it is a fact that for a long time the people had been talking of violence — of the day when they would fight the White man and win back their country — and we, the leaders of the ANC, had nevertheless always prevailed upon them to avoid violence and pursue peaceful methods. When some of us discussed this in May and June of 1961, it could not be denied that our policy to achieve a non-racial state by non-violence had achieved nothing, and that our followers were beginning to lose confidence in this policy and were developing disturbing ideas of terrorism.[10]

The question of violence occupied the center of Mandela's statement from the dock, but it was not the question which he and his antiapartheid comrades had preferred to confront. Rather, he contended, it was a question *imposed* upon them after years of non-violent struggle: "I did not plan [sabotage] in a spirit of recklessness, nor because I have any love of violence. I planned it as a result of a calm and sober assessment of the political situation that had arisen after many years of tyranny, exploitation, and oppression of my people by the Whites."[11] At issue for the court was not the motivations or rationale for armed struggle, but rather the relationship between the outlawed African National Congress and its recently formed military wing or ancillary organization, "Umkhonto we Sizwe."[12]

As Mandela made clear in his presentation, by 1962 there was no longer a question of violence versus nonviolence with respect to conditions in South Africa. Instead, the question facing the political leadership of the ANC and all other organizations challenging the apartheid state was of a different order of principle: given the *inevitability of violence* in South Africa, what role should political organizations play vis-à-vis this violence? About this more vexed question, Mandela argued:

> [We formed] Umkhonto . . . for two reasons. Firstly, we believed that as a result of Government policy, violence by the African people had become inevitable, and that unless responsible leadership was given to canalize and control the feelings of our people, there would be outbreaks of terrorism which would produce an intensity of bitterness and hostility between the various races of this country which is not produced even by war. Secondly, we felt that without violence there would be no way open to the African people to succeed in their struggle against the principle of White supremacy. All lawful modes of expressing opposition to this principle had been closed by legislation, and we were placed in a position in which we had either to accept a permanent state of inferiority, or to defy the Government. We chose to defy the law. We first broke the law in a way which avoided any recourse to violence; when this form was legislated against, and then the Government resorted to a show of force to crush opposition to its policies, only then did we decide to answer violence with violence.[13]

Mandela went to great lengths to establish that understanding the history of struggle against the racist colonial state was necessary to comprehend the vexed question of violence as the ANC confronted it in the early 1960s and the reasons why the leadership believed that this was the best and most responsible course of action for the future of the nation. He repeatedly insisted in his statement before the court that this longer history is relevant to the questions raised by this trial — even if not the expressed subject of the trial as configured within the terms of South African legal statutes and criminal codes.[14] Mandela's recording of the history of resistance was intended to establish the great lengths to which the ANC had gone to avoid moving away from its own commitment to nonviolence, despite the escalating violence of the South African state:

> For 37 years — that is until 1949 — [the ANC] adhered strictly to a constitutional struggle. It put forward demands and resolutions; it sent delegations to the Government in the belief that African

grievances could be settled through peaceful discussion and that Africans could advance gradually to full political rights. But White Governments remained unmoved, and the rights of Africans became less instead of becoming greater.[15]

Furthermore, even after the constitutional establishment of the apartheid state in 1949, this commitment to nonviolence remained, despite the criminalization of hitherto peaceful forms of constitutional protest (demonstrations, protests, strikes, etc.) and a renewed commitment to pursue various "illegal" strategies.

According to Mandela, it was following the shooting at Sharpeville in 1960, when sixty unarmed Africans were killed and the apartheid state imposed a state of emergency that the ANC's commitment to nonviolence had reached a crisis point. As an Umkhonto leaflet published just after the Sharpeville shootings announced: "The time comes in the life of any nation when there remain only two choices: submit or fight. That time has now come to South Africa."[16] With the banning of the ANC itself as an unlawful organization, the question was no longer whether to follow or break this or that law. The very existence of the organization was now illegal. Consequently it was a question of the law itself that was at issue and whether the state had any legitimacy or right to make and enforce laws. On this question, and with no small historic irony, Mandela claimed that the ANC leadership appealed to a higher source than the laws of the Republic of South Africa:

> My colleagues and I, after careful consideration, decided that we would not obey this decree. The African people were not part of the Government and did not make the laws by which they were governed. We believed in the words of the Universal Declaration of Human Rights, that "the will of the people shall be the basis of authority of the Government."[17]

It is safe to say that Mandela did not expect to convince the court of the legitimacy of his actions, but it was an opportunity for him to publicly register something of the history without which his advocacy for, and defense of, the use of violent resistance could not be understood. Mandela was predictably sentenced to life imprisonment, as were seven others. And despite his claim that the UDHR should serve as the moral basis for legitimate revolutionary action against the apartheid state, Amnesty International's leadership now had a dilemma on its hands: a prisoner of conscience who advocated the use of violence.

Human Rights and the Diminution of Politics

Despite the eloquence of Mandela's argument/defense and what on its face appeared to be the principled basis for the ANCs decision to direct and collectively organize violent resistance to the white apartheid government, Amnesty's leadership in Britain felt compelled to rethink the propriety of maintaining Mandela as a prisoner of conscience. The decision that Mandela's statement constituted an "act of advocacy for the use of violence" was not, however, made without dissent from within the nascent organization. It seems that at this juncture there was still some play within the unconditionality of the nonviolence principle. Indeed, as the first instance of the revocation of "POC" status and in light of the fairly well known brutalities of South African apartheid, the decision by the British branch of Amnesty triggered a good deal of acrimonious debate throughout the organization, which was by then operating in twelve countries. The dissension was apparently forceful enough that a decision was made in the case of Mandela's disqualification to put the matter to a vote among all Amnesty members.[18] The fact that this was the first such all-member vote, and that it remains an extremely rare phenomenon (there have only been three such votes in Amnesty's forty-nine-year history), attests to the perceived depths of the organizational crisis that the Mandela case provoked. At stake in this decision was what kind of politics and political form the organization was going to establish and cultivate. After all the voting was tabulated, a sizeable majority had decided that Amnesty should stand by the "unconditional nature" of the nonviolence principle and drop Mandela.

It would be wrong to understand this historic episode as simply a difference of opinion or principle between two political organizations, the ANC and Amnesty International, over the question of violence versus nonviolence.[19] As Mandela made clear (and as the history of the ANC bears out), the ANC did not have "any love of violence," and it was only after "all else had failed" that the leadership begrudgingly decided to advocate the careful use of violence to be orchestrated through Umkhonto. For Mandela and comrades, the decision to use violence was not derived from any abstract principle in favor of revolutionary violence; if anything the principle of nonviolence was an integral part of the organization.[20] Correlatively for Amnesty International, as Edy Kaufman, former Executive Committee member, has argued, "limiting POC status only to those who 'did not use...or advocate violence' does not imply pacifist tendencies on the part of AI." Rather, she argues, this limitation merely reflects the organization's "explicit decision not to get involved in highly politicized judgments regarding the legitimacy of the use of violence."[21] And while it is true that Amnesty's "use" provision is inviolable ("no POC may have employed violence while committing the 'offense' for which he or she is imprisoned") there is considerable latitude in their interpretation of the "advocacy" clause, and thus the nonviolence requirement is, in her terms, "not as far-reaching as it could be" (354).

At a more fundamental level, however, what this case constituted was a historic interface between two divergent forms and logics of international political practice circa 1964 (with consequences, as we will see, well beyond this conjuncture). In the case of Amnesty, what we had was an emergent organization attempting at this juncture to establish itself as a *new* kind of international advocacy group. More specifically, Amnesty tried to articulate a new consensus politic, "far wider" in the words of founder Peter Benenson, "than that of Western civilization." Such a consensus could not, however, rely upon any existing political framework, insofar as all available models, including the international institutions of the twentieth century (most notably the League of Nations and the United Nations), were seen to be deeply inscribed in a Westphalian vision of the world: upholding the supremacy and sovereignty of states. Instead, human rights activists believed that they needed to build a new consensus politics by promulgating a radical break with the statism of the past. In the words of rights activist Helen Bamber, "this was an important moment in the emergence of a new political sensibility, demanding a minimal space for the voice and the body."[22] Something of this *modus operandi* to break with the past was at work in, for example, the organization's initial selection of POCs, drawn as they were from first, second, and third world nations, as well as from capitalist, communist, and socialist states.

Still, finding a form to articulate and advance this new politic was not going to be easy. It seems that there were two different conceptions and practices of "consensus" operative in Amnesty's new political program. On the one hand, Amnesty claimed a consensus politic that involved the process of seeking and coming to general agreement among various groups or parties. This form was believed to be the manner in which the UDHR had been drafted and pertained primarily to the principles of human rights themselves as found in the Universal Declaration. The principles encoded in the Universal Declaration were to be (re)activated in minimalist (even "prepolitical") terms, on unassailable grounds, and in ways to which everyone could agree.[23] The category of the "POC" was intended, in part, to function in this manner. In general, such consensus building is believed to rely heavily on the basis of a common feeling that cuts across (before and between) ideological differences and conflicts. But this was a consensus that in the words of Amnesty's founder Peter Benenson was "all the more impressive in view of the vast (and partly irreconcilable) differences among the world religions in their understanding of reality and human destiny."[24]

On the other hand, a second sense of consensus politics was also at work in the practice of Amnesty. This second form involves what Raymond Williams has called the negative form of consensus politics, whereby "consensus" means "a policy of avoiding or evading differences or divisions of opinion in an attempt to 'secure the center' or 'occupy the middle ground.'" Such a practice, Williams argues, not only constitutes a "deliberate evasion of basic conflicts of principle" but also institutes a "process in which certain issues [are] effectively excluded from political argument."[25] This version of consensus politics seems apropos to the organizational form of Amnesty International, insofar as it was guided by the strictest principles of nonpartisanship, neutrality, objectivity, and empiricism. Here is just a sampling of these organizational principles:

1. the organization would not be funded by or otherwise linked to any party in a conflict or to any governmental entity;

2. the organization would be impartial in its criticisms, taking care to denounce abuses by governments of all political persuasions and geopolitical alignments;

3. all claims would be made on the basis of facts gathered through systematic field research and avoid any sweeping comments not sustained by empirical evidence;

4. the organization would exercise care in its use of language, avoiding, for example, references to "torture" when "mistreatment" would be more appropriate;

5. the organization would report all findings, including contradictory evidence such as conflicting testimony from government agents and individuals. . . . [26]

As we can glean from the foregoing, carving out a new discursive space ("beyond political differences") and political practice ("to which all ideological parties can adhere") required a purification process unrivaled in its scope and unequalled in its simplifications (not in a "dumb" sense, but rather in a hypermeticulous sense that entailed avoiding all manners of complexity particularly as they involve the matter of historical contingency) — an ideo-discursive space, that is, that desired nothing less than an absolute break with history.

In other words, the prisoner of conscience, through its restrictive conditions, performs a critical diminution of what constitutes "the political." The concept not only works to banish from recognition those who resort to or advocate violence, but at the same time it works to efface the very historical conditions that might come to serve as justification — political and moral — for the taking up of arms. Like the South African court that was not interested in Mandela's historical account but only in whether he was guilty of an offense of the legal code, Amnesty's investment in steering clear of "politicized judgments" reifies the antihistoricism of the Law in the name of an absolute (ahistorical) principle: nonviolence. The "success" of this politic has been enormous, but the costs have yet to be adequately exhumed. As we do know, one consequence of this winnowing of the political field includes the fact that Amnesty never found itself able "to condemn the best known legally based system of human rights violations in the world: apartheid in South Africa."[27]

Decolonization and the Politics of Revolutionary Violence

Mandela situates the move to armed struggle against apartheid in South Africa in the geohistorical context of the beginning of what he termed "a new phase in the drive for the total liberation of Africa."[28] As he wrote:

> In China, India, Indonesia, and Korea, American, British, Dutch, and French imperialism, based on the concept of the supremacy of Europeans over Asians, has been completely and perfectly exploded. In Malaya and Indo-China, British and French imperialisms are being shaken to the foundations by powerful and revolutionary

national liberation movements. In Africa there are approximately 190,000,000 Africans as against 4,000,000 Europeans.[29]

The quest for total liberation against alien, white colonial rule had reached a fever pitch throughout the continent. In 1960 alone, an unprecedented number of African nations achieved independence, including Nigeria, Senegal, Mali, Belgian Congo (Zaire, then Democratic Republic of Congo), French Congo (Republic of Congo), Ivory Coast (Côte d'Ivoire), Upper Volta (Burkina Faso), Cameroon, Somalia, Dahomey (Benin), Mauritania, Madagascar, Niger, Chad, Togo, Gabon, and the Central African Republic. These seventeen newly independent nations had wrested control from the colonizing countries of Belgium, Britain, Italy, and (the vast majority) from France. While 1960 was a watershed year in the decolonization of African nations, it was preceded in the decade before by the successful liberation of Libya (1951), Morocco (1956), Sudan (1956), Tunisia (1956), Ghana (1957), and Guinea (1958). It would be followed in short order by the independence of Sierra Leone and Tanzania (1961), Burundi, Rwanda, and Uganda (1962), Kenya and Zanzibar (1963), Malawi and Zambia (1964), Botswana and Lesotho (1966), Equatorial Guinea, Mauritius and Swaziland (1968). The rest of colonized Africa, mostly nations under Portuguese rule, would become independent in 1975 (Cape Verde, Guinea Bissau, Mozambique, and Angola), 1976 (Seychelles and Western Sahara), and 1980 (Zimbabwe). In less than thirty years a continent cast off the shackles of colonial rule. This was the *international* context within which the ANC, under the auspices of Umkhonto we Sizwe, moved into the first phase of revolutionary armed struggle.

Since the adoption of apartheid in 1949 by the National Party, black South Africans were subject to the proliferation of racist legislation and police repression. In 1950 the white government passed a series of major apartheid laws: the Immorality Act (forbidding all sexual relations between whites and nonwhites), the Population Registration Act (requiring all inhabitants of South Africa to be classified and registered according to their "racial characteristics"), the Suppression of Communism Act and the Group Areas Act (assigning racial groups to particular residential and business areas). "Mixed marriages" were also outlawed. In 1951 the government passed the Bantu Homeland Act, which denied black South Africans national citizenship; black South Africans became residents of their new "homelands" and were considered foreigners in South Africa. They were thus required to carry passports to enter. In 1952 a series of repressive "pass laws" were adopted, and scores of black Africans became subject to repeated police harassment and imprisonment. In 1953 the "separate but not necessarily equal" policy was established as law and the Bantu Education Act, which enforced the separation of races in all educational institutions, was also passed. In 1955, sixty thousand black Africans were evicted from Sophiatown in Johannesburg after the area was designated a whites-only area. In early 1960, sixty-nine unarmed black Africans were murdered in Sharpeville for protesting the pass laws. In March 1960, a state of emergency was declared and, among other things, the ANC was outlawed. In October of that year, white South Africans voted to withdraw from the British Commonwealth. The Republic of South Africa was established in 1961.

In contrast to Amnesty's articulation of a new consensus politics, the international political practice cultivated by antiapartheid activists in South Africa was deeply inscribed in the history and practice of decolonization, nearly ubiquitous across the continent of Africa as well as much of the global South. It was not coincidental that in his role as leader of the ANC, Mandela spent the year 1962, up until the time of his imprisonment in August, traveling the continent and meeting with a host of anticolonial nationalist African leaders: Nyerere (Tanganyika); Selassie (Ethiopia); Abboud (Sudan); Bourguiba (Tunisia); Ben Bella (Algeria); Keita (Mali); Senghor (Senegal); Touré (Guinea); Tubman (Liberia); and Obote (Uganda). It was, he says, during this time that he "started to make [his] study of the art of war and revolution."[30] And, as he declared in his trial statement, he "examined all types of authority on the subject [of warfare and military strategy] — from the East and from the West, going back to the classic work of Clausewitz, and covering such a variety as Mao Tse Tung and Che Guevara on the one hand, and the writings on the Anglo-Boer War on the other" (175).

The inscription of black South African armed struggle within the geohistorical context of global decolonization underscores the critical claim of the most famous theorist of decolonization, Frantz Fanon, who argued that "decolonization...is an historical process: ...it can only be understood, it can only find its significance and become self coherent insofar as we can discern the history-making movement which gives it form and substance."[31] In other words, the necessary violence of decolonization is not intelligible without understanding the historical conditions that have determined its practice nor without grasping the history-making force that is activated through the direct confrontation with death that the colonized subject risks for the sake of liberation. The very necessity of violence that Fanon insists upon, and that Mandela records in the context of the struggle against apartheid, emerges from the historical reality that there was simply no space of compromise in the colonies, no space of common feeling, no space, prepolitical or otherwise, that could serve as the basis for negotiation, and most certainly, no "depoliticized human ground on which to stand."[32] Violence and the language of pure force were the basis of the colonial enterprise — constituting the very subjects of colonization and overdetermining the politico-discursive spaces available for negotiation and contestation. In this context, as Fanon pointed out, the arrival of the discourse of nonviolence is met with critical suspicion:

> At the critical, deciding moment the colonialist bourgeoisie, which had remained silent up till then, enters the fray. They introduce a new notion, in actual fact a creation of the colonial situation: nonviolence. In its raw state this nonviolence conveys to the colonized intellectual and business elite that their interests are identical to those of colonialist bourgeoisie and it is therefore indispensable, a matter of urgency, to reach an agreement for the common good. Nonviolence is an attempt to settle the colonial problem around the negotiating table before the irreparable is done, before any bloodshed or regrettable act is committed.[33]

The decolonization struggle in South Africa, as in many other areas around the globe, had two absolutely critical targets: the colonial state and white supremacy. As disparate as the struggles against colonization were and as vexed as the question of independence was, the overthrow of the racist colonial state was a common feature of decolonization. And when Fanon wrote that this had to be a violent phenomenon, he was arguing that the colonial state would never relinquish its hold on power without intense and violent resistance. This truth was borne out over much of the world in the 1950s and 1960s, as well as the 1970s and beyond. Even a cursory glance at this history bears out that the form of decolonizing praxis required the sublation of the colonial state. The political forms developed out of such situations could not relinquish the right to use violence, even, as in the case of South Africa, where the decision to use such tactics was repeatedly deferred despite the insistent brutalities of the state.

Despite the historic dynamic driving global decolonization forward, Amnesty International sought to cultivate a different form of political action and politics. Amnesty aligned itself with the counter-revolutionary consensus established in the UDHR. Amnesty's political mission did have a certain critical relation to the state (after all, as Edward Said has written, "it is national governments acting in the name of national security who have infringed the rights of individuals and groups who are perceived as standing outside the nationalist consensus"). The advance of Amnesty's mission, however, was delimited by the transposition of the question of the political onto a decidedly antihistorical, moral plane. That is to say, like decolonization, human rights NGOs have an antagonistic relation to the state; however, adherence to the principle of nonviolence undercuts any force this position may have insofar as it shares the formal properties that underpin the supremacy of Law.

Amnesty International has had to revisit this question on numerous occasions over its history, introducing the supplementary concept of "illegal" laws and a "last resort" clause to inflect its nonviolence principle, however, the fundamental antirevolutionary thrust established at this juncture has never been undone.[34] A revolutionary politics would require taking sides, allowing for the possibility of the use of violence, etc., but an international rights politic was to become something distinct from the politics of decolonization. As a result, the discourse of human rights had little or no purchase on the realities of colonial rule and the national independence struggles to overthrow colonial states everywhere. An explicit human rights framework was thus understandably absent from the discourses of anticolonial liberation.

The inclusion of the newly independent nations of Africa and Asia in the United Nations would come to influence the production of UN resolutions asserting the "rights of colonized peoples" with, for example, the 1966 passage on the rights of all peoples to self-determination. But the newly emergent international, nongovernmental human rights discourse bypassed the central questions posed by anticolonial struggles in favor of the antirevolutionary consensus. As Richard Falk has noted about these early international citizens groups:

> The main human rights NGOs were very much outgrowths of Western liberal internationalism and looked mainly outward to identify abuses in Communist and Third World countries. In part, this reflected civilizational, as well as partisan and ideologized, orientations. It was expressed by a very selective emphasis by human rights organizations on the abuse of dissenters and political opposition or on the denial of Western-style political liberties.... In other words, human rights progress, while definitely subversive of statist pretensions in certain key respects, still remained generally compatible with the maintenance of existing geopolitical structures of authority and wealth in the world and, as such, exerted only a marginal influence.[35]

The role of the formulation of the concept of prisoner of conscience and the disqualification of Mandela should not be underestimated in either the irrelevance of human rights instruments in anticolonial struggles or the subsequent development of an NGO human rights politic "generally compatible with the maintenance of existing geopolitical structures." The constitution of a Western liberal internationalism is deeply inscribed in these formative concepts and events.[36]

Pure Politics

The politics of human rights are not simply different from other types of radical or progressive political forms; rather, the politics of human rights have come to *oppose* other progressive forms especially, but not only, when and where we fail to "discern the movements which give [them] historical form and substance." As Michel Foucault argued, "discourses of right and legitimacy are not simply ways of protecting individuals from the existence of power, but are also disciplinary practices which constitute human subjects in new relationships of power."[37] In this way we must learn to question any articulation of human rights that seeks, in the words of Wendy Brown, to "operate in an ahistorical, acultural, acontextual idiom that claims distance from specific political contexts and historical vicissitudes and thus necessarily participates in a discourse of enduring universality."[38] This is where the task of *reading* human rights becomes critical to the question of their political value and where interpretation can, in Said's formulation, "be for, rather than only about, freedom." The difficulty for political (as well as philosophical) interpretation "is how to disentangle discourse and principle on the one hand from practice and history on the other."[39]

While commentators have been content to say that the concept of the "prisoner of conscience" was entirely consistent with the principles enshrined in the Universal Declaration and therefore of no special significance or novelty, it is important to attend to all of the ways in which the category rearticulates long and complex histories of political imprisonment — a rearticulation that locates the "political prisoner" on an entirely new plane of struggle. The prisoner of conscience was not a subset of a larger category of political prisoners, but a wholly novel figure, altogether distinct in its ideological makeup and political function, and entirely disjunctive with respect to older concepts of political imprisonment. The coming into being of the prisoner of conscience with the public announcement by Amnesty's founding members marked the emergence of a new rights-bearing subject critical to the constitution of an international consensus, which more and more nation-states have been willing to sign onto. The increasing willingness to countenance the validity of the POC and other human rights categories as part of the normative architecture of world order derives from the presumption that it comes as a relatively inexpensive part of a "neo-Westphalian"[40] deal in which select rights are acknowledged in return for "respect for sovereignty" and inclusion in circuits of neoliberal, global capitalism.[41] The strategic ideo-discursive shift to the concept of the "prisoner of conscience," then, was not simply a modification in nomenclature.

To understand this requires rethinking the provision against using or advocating violence as something more than just a limiting condition(al). Such an understanding issues from recognizing the unique place that violence occupies vis-à-vis the modern state form. In the words of cultural theorist David Lloyd, "violence is what summons into being the emergence of the modern state apparatus."[42] Modern states came into being by securing a monopoly on the concentrated means of violence over a particular territory. Securing and maintaining such a monopoly is the necessary condition for the reproduction of control over the national territory. The maintenance of this monopoly resides in the capacity of the state to first distinguish, and subsequently control, the terms of "legitimate" and "illegitimate" violence within the territory. The institution of the Law has been imbued with this function within the modern nation-state. According to political theorist

Nicos Poulantzas, "law is the code of organized public violence."[43] This originary monopolization relies most forcefully on the state's ability to convert the violence of territorial conquest into legality and any resistant violence into illegality. The durability of the state form is intimately bound up with the question of the convertibility and/or nonconvertibility of violence into the structures of (il)legality.

Every modern nation-state has undergone this historic process, which does not cease upon the establishment of the state over a given territory, but must be perpetually renewed against challenges to its monopoly from within and from without. In the case of the colonial state form, however, the hegemonic functions involved in the convertibility and naturalization of (state) violence into law and (popular) violent resistance into criminality were complicated by alien rule and the racist structures of exploitation.[44] The heavy reliance of the colonial state on unadorned, brute force is evidence of the extreme difficulty of securing hegemonic consent among colonized peoples.[45]

Most critically, then, the nonviolence clause in the concept of the prisoner of conscience all-too-readily cedes the monopoly over the means of violence to the state. In its strict circumscription of what type of subjects merit protection, the concept of the prisoner of conscience performs a reification of the state's monopoly on violence as secured through Law — sanctioning the institution of the Law to carry out the enforcement of this monopoly. Hereafter the concept of human rights can be posed only within the question of the proper/improper application of the law (a procedural question). The law itself, and with it the state's capacity to make and enforce the law, is protected from contestation, outside the space of consensus politics. In Foucault's terms, "rights discourse always returns the subject to its juridical status."[46] The purifying operation implicit in the absolute exclusion of the question of violence from the politics of imprisonment may have simplified the question of the proper/improper relation between law and politics, but it came at the high cost of a radical divergence from the world-historic movement of decolonization. And more careful attention to the lessons of modern nation-state formation and the structure of colonial oppression would have shown this to be a dangerous cessation and divergence indeed.

Instead it was to the structure of Cold War contaminations of human rights discourse that activists turned for cues in the development of their technologies of purification. In the propagandistic discourse of political imprisonment between the Cold War superpowers, the impasse for human rights appeared as one of instrumentalization — wherein the United States and the Soviet Union exchanged rhetorical jabs pertaining to the existence or nonexistence of political prisoners and what this meant for their respective zones of control. In such a context, it is plausible to assume that any strategy of rearticulation would need to proceed by taking the "politics" out of the concept of political imprisonment and immunizing it as much as possible from Cold War antagonists' intent on ensnaring it, manipulating it, controlling it, and ultimately strangling it. The prisoner of conscience evidenced just such a strategy of purification while leaving unexamined and immune the excluded, contaminating structures of colonial racism and oppression. And the disqualification of Nelson Mandela served as a testament to the comparatively superficial concern to connect the consciousness of the new universality to the popular strength of revolutionary struggles of decolonization. Ironically, then, the attempts to delink human rights discourse from its Cold War contaminations wound up reinscribing it within the very institutions of the state apparatus against which it had sought an international resolution. With the sacrosanct principle of nonviolence thus upheld through the disqualification of Mandela as a prisoner of conscience, Amnesty departed the scene from which it was no longer possible to say "I don't believe in violence as a general political axiom."[47]

"Between the Anvil and the Hammer"

The vexed and complex questions surrounding the strategic use of violence were raised again and again over the course of the historic struggle against apartheid. And from 1960 with the launching of Umkhonto to the mid-1970s the ANC's position (as well as that of Mandela) was fairly firm in its insistence on the limited form of violent resistance (sabotage), on their strict guidelines about the proper targets of controlled violence (economic infrastructure), and on their directive that any action must be undertaken only after careful planning and with thorough consultation with other organizations. As part of the extensive disciplinary training of Umkhonto forces, it was impressed upon the troops that their use of violence was subordinate to a political calculus in terms of what would advance the broader goal of ending apartheid. What had been conceived of as a last resort was to remain, after some fifty-odd years, highly restricted in its deployment.[48]

By the early 1970s, however, the effects of the South African state's counterinsurgency assault had taken its toll on the ANC, with most of its leadership either dead, in prison, or in exile. Out of this political vacuum more militant, black youth–oriented groups began to gain prominence, effectively organized collectively under the umbrella organization, the Black People's Convention (BPC) headed by Steve Biko.[49] In a demonstration of the emergent organizational capacities of the new movements, thousands of schoolchildren in the Soweto township left their classrooms on June 16, 1976, in protest against the mandated use of Afrikaans as the language of instruction in black schools. By the end of that day some twenty-nine children were dead. The next day all of South Africa was ablaze. The wanton slaughter of black children put the absolute brutality of the state on full display and dramatically altered the course of debates about the need for self-defense and violent resistance. Rather than securing the hegemony of the Afrikaaner language, the events of April 1976 in Soweto ensured that the primary language of black youth instruction would henceforth be that of armed struggle. From his prison cell of more than a decade, Nelson Mandela advanced his public support for the rising tide of militancy: "between the anvil of mass action and the hammer of armed struggle we shall crush apartheid and white minority racist rule."[50]

Following the state assassination of Steve Biko on September 12, 1977, and the subsequent outlawing of all black consciousness organizations in October of the same year, it was the ANC that seized upon the opportunity to recruit the new generation of 1976. In addition to organizational contacts between the ANC and the Black People's Convention, the younger members of the Soweto generation were attracted to the ANC because of their now long-standing position in favor of the use of violence against apartheid and their capacity to provide military training. The ANC's willingness and ability to organize the youth superseded any ideological differences between the older and newer generations of activists (such as the fact that the black consciousness groups by and large rejected any role for whites in the struggle against apartheid). At the same time the youth infused the ANC with a new fighting spirit. As Pallo Jordan, who left South Africa in 1962, once described the differences between the 1976 generation and his own:

Most of us came from units inside with assignments given by the
organization at home, which we had to fulfill. Not so in '76. People
came out on their own.

In our day, organizations were legal and we held open meetings.
We were accustomed to distributing leaflets openly at the bus stops.
We would saturate neighborhoods by sticking pamphlets under doors
and in letter boxes. The worst that would happen is you got busted
for littering.

Now the illusions about legality have all been blown away. We
had to unlearn attitudes toward legal institutions. These are people
who grew up in an atmosphere of terrible repression. They come
with many skills and attitudes that are attuned to underground
work. (197)

The youths not only revived and transformed the ANC generally,
but they had a particularly profound effect on the ANCs waning
military wing, Umkhonto. By 1985 the ANC had intensified its use
of violent resistance and expanded its conception of legitimate targets. While still not aiming at "soft targets," the ANC decided it
would strike even if it meant civilian casualties:

We can no longer allow our armed activities to be determined solely
by the risk of civilian casualties. The time has come when those
who stand in solid support of race tyranny and who are its direct
or indirect instruments, must themselves begin to feel the agony of
our counterblows. It is becoming more necessary than ever for whites
to make it clear which side of the battle lines they stand. (198)

It was also in early 1985, in the midst of the expanding uprising,
that President Botha offered Mandela his release from prison if he
would renounce violence. Mandela refused.

Over the course of the decade following the Soweto rebellion,
the ANC's strategic flexibility on the question and practice of violent resistance proved successful as it once again established itself
as "the premier black political organization." Not every prominent
leader in South Africa, however, was convinced of the necessity of
violence as a critical mode of resistance to apartheid. Key members
of the black clergy, including Desmond Tutu, continued to serve as
the representatives for nonviolent advocacy. Tutu became prominent in the fight against apartheid in the early 1980s, ultimately
winning the Nobel Peace Prize in 1984 and becoming the first black
South African Anglican archbishop of Cape Town in 1986. As the
most prominent religious figure in the struggle, Tutu's moral and

strategic objections to the use of violent resistance were pivotal in the debates, especially when it came to the issue of the use of violence against black collaborators. On more than one occasion Tutu protected would-be victims from certain death by putting his body between the individual and the crowd.

However, as the eminent historian of the struggle against apartheid Steven Mufson has chronicled, by 1985 the position of the black clergy began to shift in crucial ways. As the religious leader of the UDF, Frank Chikane, was to state:

> The question of violence is not important to the people of the townships. They are confronted every day by troops in the townships. There is not a "violent option." It is the necessity of the situation. You have to defend yourself. More people say that the ANC is not doing enough. It is a logical consequence of what the state is doing to people. (99)

Indeed Chikane's change of heart had something to do with what the state was doing to him. Mufson recounts the details:

> After [Chikane's] release on bail in April 1985, ... his house and family were attacked with petrol bombs. Members of the Soweto community organized volunteers to guard the Chikane home. At the time he was preaching non-violence. "I was obliged to admit that I was only able to continue preaching non-violence because others were prepared to use violence to create this space for me." (101)

Despite increasing defections from the nonviolence camp, Archbishop Tutu in his role as international ambassador for the struggle continued to implore black South Africans to refrain from violence. At a funeral speech in July 1985 Tutu had this to say:

> I understand when people are angry or hurt and want to take it out on those we think are collaborators. But I abhor all forms of violence. I want to condemn in the strongest terms what happened in Duduza [the attempted killing of a suspected informer]. Many of our supporters around the world said then "Oh, oh. If they do those things maybe they are not ready for freedom." Let us demonstrate the discipline of people who know they are ready for freedom. At the end of the day, we must be able to walk with our heads high![51]

While Tutu remained publicly steadfast in favor of nonviolent resistance and economic sanctions as a means to pressure the apartheid government, it was not always easy to sustain the high ground of moral appeal, and even Tutu himself occasionally wearied: "It's clearer and clearer to me that the West doesn't care about black people. All they spend time on is the violence of the ANC, yet the [government's] shooting [of] children is not violence. I'm tired, very tired of the hypocrisy. I'm sick and tired of trying to persuade white people that our people don't like violence."[52]

Who Claims Modernity?

The International Frame of Sexual Recognition

> The legal violence of heterosexuality, the various ways it expands
> the cultural lexicon, enabling and supporting violence, tend to be
> positioned within the linear telos as belonging to the neocolonial.
> But...violence is intimately connected to the project of moder-
> nity, no matter where it exists. It begs the question about whether
> we are to apprehend violence as an indispensable dimension of
> democracy or dispense with the category of democracy altogether.
> — M. Jacqui Alexander,
> "Transnationalism, Sexuality, and the State"

Becoming Global

The year 1978 saw the establishment of the first "international"
gay organization at a conference of the Campaign for Homosexual
Equality in Coventry, England. An activist group, the International
Gay Association (IGA), was formed when conference participants
called on Amnesty International to take up the issue of the persecution of lesbians and gays.[1] The IGA, later renamed the International
Lesbian and Gay Association (ILGA, 1986), became the first gay
rights organization to gain consultative status as an NGO at the
United Nations in 1993.[2] In this effort to have sexual orientation rights acknowledged under international law, the ILGA was
joined in 1989 by the International Lesbian and Gay Human Rights
Commission (ILGHRC) based in San Francisco. Together these
organizations helped to make rights based on sexual orientation
the newest particularity in the universalizing human rights legacy
of the European enlightenment.

As Joseph Massad has argued of this emergent "gay international," the movement "appropriated the prevailing U.S. discourse on human rights in order to launch itself on an international scale."[3] Indeed, by the late 1980s rights discourse had become the privileged idiom out of which mainstream U.S. gay and lesbian activists and organizations increasingly sought to articulate a "new" politics of sexuality based on securing constitutional and legal protections.[4] The reorienting of sexual orientation politics toward human rights has resulted in the rearticulation of homosexuality across a vast "neoliberal network of local (the antidiscrimination ordinances and domestic partner registration provisions in any number of U.S. and Western European cities), national (the new constitutions of Ecuador and South Africa), and transnational institutions (single-issue organizations like ILGA and ILGHRC, or broader umbrella human rights organizations like Human Rights Watch or Amnesty International)."[5] In this post–Cold War rearticulation of sexual politics, rights have come to serve as an end in themselves rather than a template for the tactical mobilization of a social movement. Gone for good, it seems, are the days when groups like the Gay Liberation Front declared that they were "a revolutionary group of men and women formed with the realization that complete sexual liberation for all people cannot come about until existing social institutions are abolished."[6]

In the specific case of ILGHRC it was immigration that served as the point of entry from which to advance the claim for international sexual recognition, as this activist lobby sought reunification for lesbian and gay couples divided by nationality. And while it may be unconscionable to stand in the way of love or to oppose the flight to freedom, it is imperative in the interest of both collective desires that we also, at the same time, consider "the international homosexual movement's complicity in developmental and universalist depictions of third world sexual mores" and the consistent reproduction of imperialist axiomatics at work behind the advocacy for sexual rights as human rights.[7]

International Solidarity?

On March 22, 1994, the United States Immigration and Naturalization Service (INS) granted political asylum to a Mexican national named "José García" (alias) on the basis of sexual persecution.[8] Advocates for García, which included the International Lesbian and Gay Human Rights Commission (ILGHRC), the International Lesbian and Gay Association (ILGA), and Amnesty International (AI), hailed the decision as a "victory for democracy and freedom."[9] García's press statement, distributed to local (San Francisco), national, and international media outlets, and read at the press conference following the decision, outlined some of the terms and consequences of this victory:

> I wish to express my deepest and most heartfelt thanks to the United States government for granting me asylum. To me this country is a land of freedom where respect for human rights, for all its people, is not only preached but practiced. When I was growing up in Mexico, and as an adult there, I suffered unspeakable degradations for the sole reason that I am gay. I suffered rapes, beatings, countless humiliations. The police on numerous occasions arrested me solely because I was gay.... They extorted money from me. On one occasion, they raped me....

There were no dissenting voices present at the celebration, despite the fact that one of Mexico's oldest gay organizations, Círculo Cultural Gay (CCG, Mexico City), had expressed severe reservations about the case. According to CCG's founder Jorge Covarrubias, García's deposition was made up of "lies and gratuitous attacks" on the integrity of Mexican people and Mexico.[10] Coming from Covarrubias, such a contention was significant as he was anything but a state apologist. He criticized the two "international" human rights organizations on the grounds that their participation was damaging to the broader struggle for democracy and rights in Mexico. He argued that no international organization that claimed to be working in support of rights for gay and lesbian people should have been anywhere near this case. Nevertheless, García and his advocates had, for their part, successfully narrated him into the United States.

How do we begin to understand this rift between organizations that, by all accounts, should be working together on behalf of sexual minorities? In the interest of international solidarity, ILGHRC's Latin American program director, Jorge Cortiñas, notified Covarrubias as soon as he received word about the asylum case from García's San Francisco–based lawyer. The lawyer had contacted ILGHRC and Amnesty International and asked them to provide documentation of homosexual persecution in Mexico. Cortiñas faxed the deposition to CCG to see if they would be interested in promoting the case. Everybody recognized that the lawyer's deposition, which detailed the abuses to which García had purportedly been subject, was more than likely exaggerated or at least padded, as would be necessary to win a case of asylum. Still everyone, CCG included, was willing to consider that the case might have enough validity to warrant support and publicity.

Under the auspices of Círculo Cultural Gay, Covarrubias and his partner Jorge Fichtl had been working on gay and lesbian issues since the mid-1970s, and they were always interested in making public challenges to state-sponsored and popular violence against Mexican gays and lesbians. They had extensive contacts in the Guadalajara area where the assaults upon García were said to have taken place. One month after his initial discussion with Cortiñas, Covarrubias wrote a letter to ILGHRC informing them that the story was completely fabricated ("all of García's friends laughed when they heard the tale"). As such the case would not be of any use to *Círculo,* or ILGHRC for that matter, in their work against state and state-sanctioned violence. Cortiñas, for his part, agreed. But despite CCG's measured response to the deposition and their findings with respect to its veracity, ILGHRC leadership decided to go ahead with support for the case. ILGHRC provided information to the lawyer to substantiate the claims that García's experiences were not unique to him alone and that he would likely never be safe as long as he resided in Mexico.

ILGHRC, it seems, had a great deal invested in its recently formed Sexual Asylum Project and would not have its mission interrupted despite objections from one of the two main gay organizations operating at the time in Mexico (the other being Colectivo Sol). Cortiñas did, however, question the logic of blatantly ignoring the concerns and findings of *Círculo,* but he was overruled. Sexual asylum cases had become the centerpiece for the nascent organization, with more than fifty pending at the time of the García decision. Moreover, such cases were considered popular with prospective contributors. The Christmas fundraising mailer for 1994 (the year of García's asylum case) used a picture of a young man from Turkey, awarded asylum earlier in the year, accompanied by a letter written by a direct-mailer marketing agent in the voice of the successful asylee:

> My name is _____, and 4 years ago at the age of 17, I was beaten and assaulted by a Turkish police officer in a park in Istanbul... because I was gay. Nicknamed "AIDS" by my classmates, disowned

> by my family, and suicidal, I fled Turkey.... In October, I was granted
> political asylum to the U.S. My attorney won the case ... because
> of critical documentation provided by ILGHRC detailing the every-
> day persecution of homosexuals in Turkey.... Your past support of
> ILGHRC made it possible for me to be celebrating this holiday sea-
> son in freedom and safety.... And so I hope that you will contribute
> to ILGHRC's life-saving work so that next year another 17-year-
> old, somewhere in the world, will also be safe and free, instead of
> enduring the nightmare that I so narrowly survived.

This letter was also subject to objections from particular staff
members at ILGHRC, but this time concerns about celebrating
U.S. freedom and safety over and against tyrannies elsewhere were
overridden on the grounds that "such letters work."[11] Here, the
epistemic violence of the international mission is capitalized on by,
and to, the letter.

I do not cite these "narratives of persecution" to suggest that they
are always and in every detail false or that violence against persons
for their sexual practices or gendered mannerisms or appearance
never occurs or should be ignored. Rather I want to emphasize that
as asylum narratives they are subject to mediations, conventions,
and codes that underwrite the power of the United States to prescribe the script of human rights.[12] The deposition, the fundraising
letter, and sexual asylum narratives in general posit with unwavering regularity the third world individual as living within a nation of
danger and the first world rescuers as residing in a space of safety
and enlightened freedom. Such a third world individual must be represented as desiring a freedom located in those nations which have
the power to grant, by their good graces and superior weapons,
spaces of democracy and freedom. Statements must conform to a
logic that bifurcates the world in that grim prose of power that has
long distinguished the "West from the rest." The saved subject does
not speak; rather the grateful subject is used to voice the myth of
a Manichean world comprised of nations of safety and nations of
danger.

While the victim could not speak, García himself could. Soon
after the press conference he told Cortiñas that the rape by the Mexican police was a revised version of the story he had originally given
to the lawyer. In the predeposition account García had said that he
was subject to sexual assault at the hands of state authorities, only
it was not by Mexican police officers, but instead by INS officials
on the U.S. side of the border. This part of the story, which would

have complicated any simple national binary, had to be relocated and revised (if not expunged) to fit a script that insists upon a strict and absolute difference between first and third world nations. The excited willingness on the part of some North American gay and lesbian rights activists to reproduce this repetitive drama of democracy and barbarity in order to extend our rights-based agenda in "America" is not without severe costs in an international frame. Ignoring *Círculo's* objections may have helped to win García's asylum case, and it may have helped raise money for the international mission of ILGHRC, but at the same time, it raises serious questions about the type of "international politics" that underwrite the globalizing practice of gay and lesbian human rights.

The geopolitical lesson underwritten by the narrative for sexual asylum was dutifully consumed by the press corps in attendance at the victory celebration of José García. Not wanting to miss an opportunity to probe more deeply into the heart of darkness, one reporter queried: "What are conditions like for gays and lesbians in the rest of Latin America?" To which the Amnesty International representative with a global mission was quick to respond: "We have reports that torture, rape, and extra-judicial punishments are daily occurrences, not only in Mexico, but all throughout Latin America." The script of absolute difference was summarily completed (with an exclamatory gasp) in the coded binary of democratic and barbaric nations — specific to the United States and Mexico in this case, but apparently applicable to any country south of the Rio Grande.

Both the García case and the fundraising letter evidence the persistence of a stark, imaginary geopolitical divide between first and third worlds, democratic and barbaric nations. The narratives are readily intelligible because they restage a by-now familiar story: the backwardness of the third world and the benevolence of the first world. Danger there, safety here. Victims there, saviors here. Tyranny there, freedom here, and so on. The involvement of ILGHRC raises critical questions about the willingness of first world human rights activists to reproduce such frames even when facing objections from potential allies in the South. Was noninvolvement possible? Was this the only way to narrate García out of the third world and into the first? Does the human rights framework refuse any narrative mode of entry that does not conform to a tendentious geopolitical logic of democratic and barbaric nations? Is the human rights activist hopelessly condemned to reproduce the contaminated scripts of victim and savior, tyranny and freedom? Perhaps. But at the very least, following the formulation of George Yúdice, it calls into question "the authority of U.S. intellectuals and activists...to represent other peoples, especially when the injunction to do so stems from our own internal identity politics."[13]

Uncapitalizable Tragedies

García and his lawyer presented a graphic biographical account that chronicled a persistent series of physical abuse — rapes by his father and Mexican police authorities, harassment by his schoolmates, forced prostitution from which he was to have contracted HIV, etc. — over the course of his life in Guadalajara. In themselves, however, these events would not be sufficient to warrant sexual asylum to the United States. What had to be established was that he would be in danger no matter where he resided in Mexico. For evidence of this, ILGHRC provided García's lawyer with a report that focused on two series of multiple murders which had occurred in recent years in Tuxtla Gutiérrez (1991–93) and Mexico City (1992).

Between June 1991 and February 1993 at least fifteen *travestis* were murdered in and around Tuxtla Gutiérrez, the capital of Mexico's southernmost state, Chiapas.[14] All of the killings were carried out with high-caliber weapons "reserved for the exclusive use of the Mexican army and the federal and state judicial police."[15] The police contended, for as long as they could, that the murders were "crimes of passion" carried out by jealous and jilted lovers.[16] Sensationalist newspapers echoed these claims, producing numerous stories about lavish parties, orgies, and transvestite prostitutes, all the while speculating as to the sick homosexual murderer behind the mystery. Public officials used the police and press accounts as a pretext to intensify harassment against *travestis* and gay men in the city, closing down the two most popular nightclubs, "Sandy's Bar" and the "Latin Lover" in July and September 1992. What was missing from these lurid speculative accounts, among other relevant facts, was that in October 1990, Patrocino González Garrido, governor of the state of Chiapas, promulgated a new "public health law," which prohibited cross-dressing in public. And then, in the midst of the string of killings, Governor González Garrido publicly declared that "the gay community is unnatural, and violates all concepts of ethics, hygiene, and normality."[17]

The public health law, the closing of the bars, and perhaps the murders themselves were all part of a generalized program of *travesti* eradication (despite the cynical official claim that closing the bars was to "protect the gays"). The popular stage shows afforded the *travestis* with a critical source of income. According to one of the *travesti* workers, the bar closing had a predictable outcome:

> We had to go to the street, this was the only thing we could do. Well, there are some who worked as stylists, and others who have some job, but for those who didn't they had to go to the street.[18]

Despite how dangerous downtown Tuxtla had become in recent months for *travestis,* many were forced back to work in the streets to make a living. The *travestis* regarded the danger as coming squarely from the police: "transvestites are very well known and accepted, it is seen as something quite common, people are not scandalized. Policemen are the ones making a lot of noise about it. They are after the money."[19]

In mid-1992, one of the young *travestis* in Tuxtla, Neftalí Ruiz Ramírez, contacted *Círculo Cultural Gay* about the murder and disappearance of a couple of his friends. After meeting with Ruiz and a few of the others who were willing to talk about what was going on, Covarrubias and Fichtl began to mount a campaign to draw attention to the murders. The campaign would ultimately involve the publication of a letter in every major Mexico newspaper signed by more than two hundred prominent intellectuals and public figures, organized marches in both Tuxtla and Mexico City, and even a public pronouncement from the Department of Human Rights of the Archdiocese of Mexico City, which stated that "we have strong evidence that makes us believe this [antigay] campaign has been waged by various police agencies, with the possible involvement of the army."[20] For whatever reasons, the killings appear to have ceased in early 1993.[21] Most critically, in the context of international human rights, Covarrubias's initial attempts to solicit the support of ILGHRC and the United Nations were largely unsuccessful. From ILGHRC, *Círculo* received a letter of sympathy replete with an apology that there was "unfortunately" little they could do. No response was received from the United Nations.

The twin assault on life and livelihood continued throughout late 1992 and into 1993 despite mounting public pressure and condemnation. Such publicity did, however, necessitate a shift in tactics:

the police now turned their attention to producing a killer. *Travestis* were brought in as suspects and/or possible informants after which, many reported being told that they too would be killed "if they continued acting like women."[22] In January 1993, the press was notified that the police had caught their man, Martín Moguel, the former lover of one of the murdered *travestis*, Rodrigo Bermúdez Padilla ("La Tatiana"). Moguel had been tortured, shown pictures of his four-year-old daughter, and forced to sign a "confession" that he was the *hired* murderer in a plot organized by Germán Jiménez Gómez, a former federal deputy of the ruling Partido Revolucionario Institucional (PRI).[23] This cynical attempt to produce a killer was repeated a month later with the arrest and torture of Carlos Cruz Bautista. Moguel and Jiménez were to stand trial in February, Cruz in June.

Neftalí Ruiz Ramírez ("Vanesa") had seen the men who picked up "La Tatiana" and "La Gaby" the night before their dead bodies were found, and Moguel, Ruiz claimed, was not one of the men. Ruiz had been very active in publicly denouncing the murders, and he also played a prominent role in organizing the first march to protest the killings in October 1992 in Tuxtla Gutiérrez. He was scheduled to testify on Moguel's behalf when, on February 6, ten days before the trial was to begin, the twenty-two-year-old from Villacorzo was gunned down while standing on a downtown street corner. According to eyewitness reports, "the individual who fired the shot worked for the State Judicial Police." Evidence that the weapon used to kill Ruiz was a state-issued 38mm caliber gun further corroborated such accounts. With the murder of Ruiz, despite the inconsistencies in the "confession" and the fact that it was extracted under torture, Moguel was found guilty and sentenced to sixteen years in prison for three of the murders, including that of his former lover. Charges against Jiménez were unexpectedly dropped soon after the trial began when doubts about the elaborate plot began to appear in local newspapers. Martín Moguel entered the state prison in San Cristóbal de las Casas to begin serving sixteen years for crimes he did not commit.

Fortunately, after the EZLN (the Zapatistas) launched an uprising in January 1994, there was a shakeup in the administration of justice in Chiapas. How long it would last and how substantive the changes remained to be seen, but in fairly rapid succession Moguel's sentence was revoked and he was released on February 4, 1994. This was followed by Cruz's release at the end of March.

After the uprising, Ignacio Flores Montiel, former coordinator of the Chiapas security forces and special investigator appointed in November 1992 by the attorney general to head the investigation into the *travesti* murders, was detained and accused of arms trafficking, kidnapping, and murder. And in April 1994, Ramón Herrera Bautista, former regional subcommander of the Chiapas State Judicial Police, was accused of forced entry and illegal detention. Moguel had identified Herrera Bautista as his torturer. The aperture created by the EZLN would subsequently be closed and no one would be charged with the murders, but at least the two men wrongly sentenced were freed.

The Dead as Narrative Backdrop

ILGHRC would commit no resources to bring publicity to these events as they were unfolding. In part, this lack of involvement resulted from the fact that the organization's Latin American division had been ill- and under-formed since their inception, given their "almost exclusive early emphasis on Eastern Europe."[24] The most common rejoinder to charges of indifference, however, was that there was simply a lack of resources available to commit to every case of violence against gays and lesbians around the world. But a lack of resources may not have been the only reason for ILGHRC's heartfelt but inactive response. To understand what may have been at work, subsequent events prove illuminating. In July 1992, after more than eleven *travesti* murders in Tuxtla, a prominent gay activist and wealthy doctor, Francisco Estrada, was found strangled to death in his Mexico City home. Five other affluent gay men were found murdered in like manner over a one-week period. The death of Estrada, who had established the first AIDS organization in Mexico City, "Ave de México," caught the attention of the gay press in North America and Europe.

ILGHRC and the International Lesbian and Gay Association (ILGA) immediately (in the absence of any request) formed a public campaign to denounce the murders of the gay men in Mexico City. In the press reports put out by ILGHRC, the murder of Estrada was featured along with the mention of the "homophobic murders of more than 15 gays in the State of Chiapas, Mexico."[25] This use of the *travesti* murders as a supplementary backdrop was the first public statement made by ILGHRC on the killings in Tuxtla.

It seems that almost overnight the value of the lives of those systematically slaughtered with police-issued bullets found currency within the narrative of international lesbian and gay human rights. The lives, that is, of Raúl Rodolfo Velazco (age twenty-two); Raúl Corzo Cruz (age thirty-five); Rodrigo Bermúdez Padilla (Tatiana, age nineteen); Freddy Chacón Rodríguez (age eighteen); Roque Jiménez Quevedo; Eredín Yaben Arreola (age twenty-one); Martín Ordoñez Vásquez (age twenty-one); Miguel Angel Gerónimo Segura (Alejandra, age eighteen); Jordán Balbuena Gómez (age twenty-five); José Luis Domínguez Hernández (Verónica, age twenty-one); Miguel López Agustín; Victor Hugo Suárez Castillejos (La Gaby, age twenty-three); Vicente Torres Toledo (La Chentilla, age twenty-five); Jorge Darinel Maldonado (age twenty-four); and Neftalí Ruiz Ramírez (La Vanesa).[26]

The devalued dead entered the discourse of international human rights in a belated and tangential fashion, as a narrative supplement to the murder of the cosmopolitan middle/upper class gay subjects. In the discourse of international gay and lesbian rights, it was the sum of the hitherto ignored lives that were appropriated and transformed, overnight, into narrative commodities to be exchanged in media markets as spectacles that evidence the necessity of the global mission. The epistemic violence reproduced here cannot be undone by the beneficence of an imperial mission under any name, but that it takes place under the rubrics of rights and freedom should alert us to the histories of violence which subtend the narrative triumph of democracy. The privileging of certain gay subjects, bourgeois and cosmopolitan, contributes to the reproduction of a class split within homosexual subcultures, rather than serving as a bulwark against the violence of state and local (hetero)sexisms. In other words, the class politics submerged within the terms of universal gay rights may, albeit unwittingly, serve to exacerbate the violence against sexual minorities who do not fit or conform to sanctioned models of modern/bourgeois/cosmopolitan gay and lesbian subjectivity. If this is the case, then our understanding of the role of ILGHRC and of the North American–led international gay rights movement, and our relation to events south of the border, would no longer be that of external savior who enters after the fact of death to champion the cause of the victim, but as always already involved in the production and policing of classed subjectivities that facilitate the *estructuración* of hierarchical antagonisms within sociosexual fields, at home and abroad.

Thus, rather than asking, "Is there another way for them to enter the first world?" we should ask "is there another way for us to enter the third world?" Given the apparent regularity with which the human rights text tends to reproduce the imperialist troping of democratic and barbaric nations and the class determinants of value, it may be that we have to think the question of human rights not as the *terminus* of repression, but as the point at which social control is reconfigured to distinguish those who are protected (and thus have rights) from those who fall on the other side of the new class apartheid. Rather than running the murders of *travestis* in the state of Chiapas and middle-class gay men in Mexico City together, as we do when we cast these killings as singular expressions of "homophobia," we must attend to, among other things, the way that class divisions, class position, and value structure the field of (inter)national sexual politics.[27] Counterarticulations of rights are hard to come by from within the texts of international human rights practice, insofar as the practical demands of activism are presumed to augur against questioning the value of human rights themselves. And yet, this is precisely what we are enjoined to do, if we hope to avoid reproducing the axiomatic structures of missionary imperialism. With this injunction in mind, I want to turn away from the field of human rights proper, in order to shift the debate away from any practical immediacy for which noninvolvement appears out of the question.[28] That is to say, as long as the question of the value of human rights is posed as one of "saving" this or that individual or as condemning the murderous violence of the state, we cannot not want to do so. Thus our ability to analyze the utility and value of human rights is predicated in part on finding analytic modes of entry through which the field of practical politics, as constituted through histories of liberal benevolence, does not always already foreclose upon the possibility of another approach.

Recognition in an International Frame

What unifies the disparate events and cultural narratives discussed thus far in this chapter is the play of recognition and nonrecognition that attend to their appearance, reappearance and disappearance in/from the language of international human rights: Will an event appear? How does it appear? What determines its mode of appearance? etc. In the field of human rights, there is perhaps no more important set of questions, given that the power of human rights resides in the business of making visible acts of extreme cruelty. Such a political practice emanates from the dominant ideological structure of North American gay politics (post-Stonewall, 1969) in which becoming visible and demanding one's rights are figured as the quintessential liberatory act.[29] Trying to ascertain the reasons why this or that event became of "public interest," the scope and scale of that interest, or why it failed to generate any interest at all, goes a long way toward developing strategies intended to bring about recognition and, presumably, promote more effective human rights action.

Let's then recast the foregoing account by outlining the primary dimensions of (non)recognition at work in each instance. The press conference produced a certain type of recognition for José García, ILGHRC, Amnesty International, and the law firm that handled the case, as well as for Mexico and the United States. The terms within which this juridical recognition was accessed were made through the reproduction of an imperial narrative sharply distinguishing the first world from the third world. Those who objected, such as *Círculo,* were not present and their objections were not made public (or recognized) by those who were there. Thus any meaning that might have been assigned to the activist rift could not take place insofar as *Círculo* did not have the capacity or force to enter into circuits of "international" recognition. Any contradictory elements were purged from the asylum script. The public consecration of United States democracy went off without a hitch.

The case of the young man from Turkey was made visible in a way that also relied upon the dominant ideological frame of the United States as benevolent savior (and charitable donors as critical rescuers), but it was made to perform this visible function in order to raise private funds for the gay and lesbian organization to carry on its mission across the globe. The limited visibility of the Turkish case had a currency in wealthy private donor markets, but nevertheless relied upon the same narrative tropes for success as were used in the courts and before the media. This suggests that there is believed to be a homologous relation between the law and public opinion. In contrast, the murders of the *travestis* in Tuxtla were, in turn, largely invisible in late 1991 and the early months of 1992 (even local papers didn't cover the killings initially). When local papers did finally take up the story, it was in grossly sensationalist terms. Once Covarrubias and CCG were called in, they were able to generate some national attention, especially in Mexico City (including the publication in the major dailies of a letter signed by some two hundred intellectuals). Local visibility, in turn, was heightened when Neftalí Ruiz Ramírez led a protest march in Tuxtla in October 1992. ILGHRC, ILGA and Amnesty International, offered no help, at least initially, in making the murders visible to wider international audiences. Again, this is no small unwillingness given that much of international human rights work consists in making systemic events/abuses visible. The whole point of trying to access the circuits of international human rights is to mobilize publicity — there is no supposition that such agencies can do anything more than that (more on the strategic politics of visibility in chapter 3). Later, however, following the murder of the physician in Mexico City, this would change, and the *travestis* would now enter the discourse of international human rights, but largely as an aggregated body intended to signify a generalized barbarity assigned to the country of Mexico.

Why certain events become hypervisible, for example, and others fail to register at all in broad public discourses is always a complicated and historically contingent question. Calculating the potential interest in an event is a notoriously difficult thing to do, insofar as it is not an entirely objective calculus. But did the events around the García case, the murders in Tuxtla and Mexico City, etc., have to become visible in the way that they did? What else, if anything, could have been done? We know that the play of (non)recognition is not random; it is regulated by an imperial divide. But we also know that the play of (non)recognition is not *wholly* controlled by any particular agents or institutions, even if power is in no way distributed evenly. Now if we bring this analysis to bear on the murders, the press conference, and this essay, we can see both the difficulties and possibilities in our concluding question.

The initial nonresponse of ILGHRC and ILGA and, perhaps, Amnesty International, with respect to the *travesti* murders evidences a certain process of calculation which assumes that the future is more or less determined and therefore it was pointless to commit limited resources to a cause that had no chance of generating widespread concern. That is to say, it is quite likely that ILGHRC believed that an international division of value from the global gay north precluded them from being able to generate any interest in the killings of *travestis* in southern Mexico. In other words, ILGHRC calculated that the North American white gay liberal (their primary supporter base) would remain indifferent to these murders given the predominance of a classist, racist, sexist, and imperialist value structure. If that is the case, and in all my discussions with activists from the agency I am led to believe this was a key reason for nonaction, then it was not a matter of the activist contingent being indifferent to the murdered *travestis;* rather it was a matter of ILGHRC's leadership calculating that their base (largely white and middle class) had been formed through a(n) (inter)national ideological framework that effectively and determinatively devalues certain lives south of the border.

Here, then, we run up against one of the critical aporias of international human rights activism. Perhaps it is one of those "positional aporias" about which Barbara Harlow has said that "neither delicacy nor development has provided uncompromised, politically absolved answers."[30] While it would be difficult to argue with the calculation that ILGHRC's primary support base would in fact be interested in helping stop the murders of *travestis* in Chiapas, the failure to challenge that supporter base ensures that the human rights agency will necessarily reproduce the dominant value-codings, while at the same time negate any unpredictability that issues from those structures being in-history. As long as the field of practical politics is configured by human rights activists and organizations in a short-term urgent rescue mode they (and we) are doomed to reproduce the contaminated structures of value that overdetermine the play of (non)recognition in an international frame. What the foregoing analysis demonstrates is that an international politics of rescue consistently reproduces an international division of humanity and works against the formation of a truly international practice of solidarity. Fortunately, in the context of Chiapas, the nation of Mexico, and the Americas more generally, an-Other politics of solidarity was in the making.

The Long March to Emancipation

Some twelve years after the beginning of the rebellion in Chiapas, the EZLN launched what the peasant rebels called "la Otra Campaña." Unlike their initial military campaign of 1994 in which they successfully seized vast amounts of territory in the rural regions of Chiapas, the Other Campaign was designed to open up a new kind of space for leftist organizing and national solidarity. Without the spectacular armed takeover of territory, the Other Campaign received comparably little international attention. It did however generate a great deal of interest in Mexico, timed as it was to coincide with the presidential campaigns of the candidates from the PRD, the PRI and the PAN. In the Zapatistas' terms, the anti-electoral campaign, fronted in this case by Delegado Zero (aka Subcomandante Marcos), was a wholly novel attempt to "construct or reconstruct another way of practicing politics." While this undertaking had no precedent in the annals of Mexican politics, it was not without its militant antecedents insofar as this new way of practicing politics was to be conducted "in the spirit of serving others, without material interests, with sacrifice, with dedication, with honesty, a way that keeps its word, or, that is to say, in the same way that militants of the left — who were not stopped by violence, jail, or death, and much less with offers of dollar bills — have done it." But while such a campaign departed from traditional electoral politics, predicated as it was not on making promises or purchasing votes (as was the tradition under the seventy-year hegemonic rule of the PRI), it was also distinctive within the annals of left politics.

In the Sixth Declaration of the Lacandón Jungle (June 2005), the CCRI (the Revolutionary Indigenous Clandestine Committee) publicly invited all political and social organizations "of the left that are not registered with any government, and individual people who believe in the resurrection of the left that do not belong to political parties recognized by the state to meet with us...to organize a national campaign, to visit every possible corner of the country, to listen and organize the word of our people." The public invitation went out to a complex, heterogeneous mass comprised of "the indigenous, the workers, the farmers, the students, the housewives, the neighbors, the small property owners, the small businesspersons, the retired, the handicapped, the religious men and women, the artists, the intellectuals, the youths, the women, the elders, the homosexuals and lesbians, the boys and girls." The campaign would, it was hoped, begin to create the dialogic space for a new kind of national network (and international model), for those of an ideological community "from below and to the left." Despite the sweeping scope of the invitation, the campaign was not open to everyone, as Marcos made clear in an exchange with an earnest young student who asked whether the invitation should be extended to all people, including people on the Right. To this suggestion, Marcos said, "No." Unsatisfied with the apparently antihumanist limits to solidarity, however, the questioner pressed on: "We need to break down walls because we are all human beings." To which Marcos was reported to reply: "Yes, we are all human beings, but some are sons of bitches and some aren't. That's the truth."[31]

In its sweeping, but not unlimited, call for mass participation from both organized and unorganized sectors and from individuals and groups whose social identities, affiliations, and affinities went far beyond any traditional models of class or peasant organizing, the rebels from the mountains of the Mexican Southeast were attempting to articulate a new kind of revolutionary collectivity. As Subcomandante Marcos had described it a few years earlier, the need for such a new kind of politics was necessary to overcome the limits of the developmentalist models that had hitherto dominated leftist organizing in Latin America:

> Broadly speaking, there were two major gaps in the movement of the revolutionary left in Latin America. One of them was the indigenous peoples, from whose ranks we come, and the other was the supposed minorities. Even if we removed our balaclavas we would not be a minority in the same way that homosexuals, lesbians, transsexuals are. These sectors were not simply excluded by the discourses of the Latin American Left of those decades — and still current today — but the theoretical framework of what was then Marxism-Leninism disregarded them, indeed took them to be part of the front to be eliminated. Homosexuals, for example, were suspect as potential traitors, elements harmful to the socialist movement and state. While the indigenous peoples were viewed as a backward sector preventing the forces of production... blah, blah, blah. So what was required was to clean out these elements, imprisoning or re-educating some and assimilating others into the process of production, to transform them into skilled labour — proletarians, to put it in those terms.[32]

In the context of this book, we should recognize that this formulation carries within it the possibility for a very different kind of politico-epistemological mapping of violence directed toward sexual minorities than that found in the identitarian frameworks of the gay north. It is not the logic of homophobia that is identified as organizing violence against gays and lesbians, *travestis* and others — a logic that circumscribes the understanding of such violence in a narrowly construed sexual plane — but rather such violence is figured through the ideological-material practices of elimination whose logic emanates from the privileging of economic productivity (encompassing both capitalist and socialist revolutionary variants). In this conceptual grid, the logic of production cuts across "right and left" ideological antagonists in such ways as to cast the indigenous as a backward impediment to development and the homosexual as a nonreproductive drag on the advancement of the proletariat. Thus Marcos argues for a relation of affinity and potential solidarity between the indigenous and homosexual sectors under the sign of those collectivities who are forcibly exteriorized from the logos of productivity.

The prospect of a new kind of politics with its new relations of affinity seems to have resonated quite profoundly with *travestis* and gays and lesbians throughout Mexico as their participation in La Otra Campaña was pronounced in every metropolitan area visited. All in all some 55 leftist organizations, 103 indigenous organizations, 162 social organizations, 453 NGOs, and thousands of individuals representing families, neighborhoods, and communities signed onto the Other Campaign within months of the publication of the Sixth Declaration, while tens of thousands more participated in the various forums held from the Suchiate to the Rio Bravo. And when the long march wound its way to the capital, and the Zapatista spokesperson made his way to the Zócalo (like the rebels' namesake Emiliano Zapata had during the revolution of 1910), delegate zero was accompanied by a large contingent of *travestis* with whom he walked arm-in-arm. As the Uruguayan journalist Raul Zibechi asks of this curious development: "what purpose is there, in classic revolutionary logic, in covering thousands of kilometers to meet with a handful of whores and crossdressers?"[33]

The group of transvestites and prostitutes who accompanied Marcos around Mexico City were from a loosely organized association called the Mexican Sex Network. The origins of this collective network date back to early 1992 when a small group of sociology graduate students from UNAM launched the Brigada Callejera de Apoyo a la Mujer (Women's Supportive Street Brigade). For more than fifteen years now the Network has been growing to the point where they have affiliates in twenty-eight of the thirty-two states of Mexico. The ideological basis for the Network centers around the idea that sex workers are persons whose labor and lives should be respected — a demand for recognition and dignity that is in contrast to the notion that all sex workers are victims who have fallen into some sort of immoral profession by virtue of ignorance, poverty, and exploitation. While members of the Network recognize that sex trafficking is a widespread problem and that sexual exploitation is a danger, they insist that such work is also a means of survival that they have chosen, given the relative dearth of economic opportunities. Indeed the affirmative relation that the workers had to their work was something that the founding members of the organization had to adjust to over the years, as co-founder Jaime Montejo recounts: "We don't agree with sex work, but it exists and will continue to exist, and in the meantime we have to do something. We were an abolitionist group, but later saw that it wasn't about saving anybody, but really about working together."[34]

What you have emerging out of this particular dialectic of decolonizing praxis is a decidedly different and altogether novel movement for political sovereignty and recognition — a new kind of organized struggle, born in the wake of the EZLN uprising after initial plans to seize the state had to be abandoned. In this context, the Other Campaign can be understood as the most recent strategic rearticulation of the Zapatista movement in response to the deadening and deadly conditions of geographic and military containment by the Mexican state. To what extent and in what ways this (historically contingent) non-state-centered movement can connect with and help advance popular insurgencies throughout the Americas remains a project-in-the-making.[35] But perhaps we should pause here, slow the pace a bit (after all indigenous struggles have been ongoing for more than five hundred years) and appreciate just how much is already powerful in these movements with their grand titles ("against neo-liberalism and for humanity") and sometimes awkward questions ("do you go by he or she?").[36] These are movements, for lack of a better word, that have only begun to recognize one another on that long march to emancipation.

3

A Duty to Intervene

On the Cinematic Constitution
of Subjects for Empire
in *Hotel Rwanda* and *Caché*

In his classic work *The Wretched of the Earth,* anticolonial theorist
Frantz Fanon argued that the international recognition of repression
and brutality in the colonies was largely determined by the presence
or absence of imperialist competition in a given area at a particular
time. Where these geopolitical turf wars were minimal or absent,
mass slaughters remained on "the other side" of the international
division of visibility:

> In 1945 the 45,000 dead at Sétif [Algeria] could go unnoticed; in
> 1947 the 90,000 dead in Madagascar were written off in a few lines
> in the papers; in 1952 the 200,000 victims of the repression in Kenya
> were met with relative indifference.[1]

The massacre at Sétif took place just before the beginning of the
Nuremberg trials as the West sought to address barbarity in its midst
while continuing to ignore long histories of racist colonial violence
outside the West. In stark contrast, when and where Cold War competition was acute, Fanon argued that even the most minor act of
repression in the colonies registered at the level of the international:

> Two men are beaten up in Salisbury and an entire bloc goes into
> action, focuses on these two men and uses this beating to raise the
> issue of Rhodesia — linking it to the rest of Africa and every colonized
> subject. (35)

It was neither the magnitude nor the form of brutality that determined the recognition of colonial violence by the West, but rather

43

the visibility was regulated through a brute calculus of racism and imperialist geopolitics.

Fanon's critical response to the imperialist world was not to point out the hypocrisies and contradictions in order to appeal to the "goodwill of European governments" (61–62). Rather, the impasse necessitated the adoption of a political program in the only language that the West recognized: *force*. Thus he affirmed anticolonial warfare and gave reasons why it was necessary:

> In its bare reality, decolonization reeks of red-hot cannonballs and bloody knives. For the last can be the first only after a murderous and decisive confrontation between the two protagonists. This determination to have the last move up to the front, to have them clamber up (too quickly, say some) the famous echelons of an organized society, can only succeed by resorting to every means, including, of course, violence. (2–3)

In this strategic formulation, Fanon rejects the solution offered by the "colonialist bourgeoisie," which at "the critical, deciding moment... introduce a new notion, in actual fact a creation of the colonial situation: non-violence" (23).

Since Fanon's death in 1961, the attainment of independence by many nations of Africa, and the end of the Cold War, a new institutional force has emerged to challenge the relative monopoly of powerful nation-states over the international borders of in/visibility: nongovernmental human rights organizations (NGOs). Beginning with the establishment of Amnesty International in 1960, the publicizing of "human rights abuses" has been taken on by an ever-widening cast of international NGOs including the Organization for Human Rights, Human Rights Watch, Oxfam, Terre des Hommes, and Médecins sans Frontières, to name but a few. Given the lack of institutional mechanisms to enforce a *legal* obligation for states to respond, human rights organizations have adopted a host of visibility strategies designed to appeal to the *conscience of the West*. The strategic circuit favored by human rights NGOs moves from (1) making conditions of violence visible to (2) provoking shame to (3) necessitating a response. In this political program, it is the ethos of shame that constitutes the critical means of challenging the narrow calculus of imperialist interest that otherwise regulates the in/visibility of conditions of violence outside the West. Such a strategic project serves as the modus operandi for the human rights practice of the major international NGOs. As Peter Takirambudde, regional director for Human Rights Watch, Sub-Saharan Africa, recently outlined:

> We seek to target those institutions that have the most influence over the recipient countries in terms of foreign aid. Part of the strategy is obviously that we seek to shame those who commit the primary abuses. But we also seek to shame those who support them, those who cooperate with them, and those who give them financial and other means of assistance. With this pressure on national and international decision-makers we seek to change abusive practices and also avoid new abuses.[2]

And indeed, since the early 1960s these agencies and institutions have developed an impressive battery of strategies to breach the international division of invisibility as it was hitherto constituted through the optics of Cold War superpower interests.

By the mid-1970s a number of factors began to coalesce that facilitated the growing prominence of human rights visibility, including the promotion of the rhetoric of human rights by the Carter administration. A major boost on the NGO-side came in 1979 when the Ford Foundation provided $500,000 of seed money to Robert Bernstein to form the group Helsinki Watch, which became Human Rights Watch in 1982. Bernstein was president of the publishing giant Random House, and he was joined, along with a cast of lawyers, by university presidents from the University of Chicago, MIT, and Columbia, as well as representatives of the literary world, such as E. L. Doctorow, Toni Morrison, and Robert Penn Warren. These institutional developments greatly enhanced and solidified the human rights strategy of pursuing media coverage and increased visibility.[3]

The networks developed and the strategies deployed by human rights NGOs have had a modest but important effect on the field of international visibility. Human rights advocacy and organizations have played an increasingly important role in turning the media's attention to conditions of violence that might otherwise have been ignored or remained largely invisible. According to media analyst Roger Kaplan, "NGOs have [succeeded] through elaborate and effective lobbying and communication strategies to disseminate their findings and through defining angles to stories that will attract media interest, such as a personal or emotive angle." "In fact," he argues, "some human rights organizations have become such effective operators, that the media use them as a source on the majority of human rights stories."[4] In an ironic reversal of historic dependency, it is the Western media that has become increasingly reliant upon NGOs for their international coverage, especially in the contexts of catastrophe and crisis. In BBC correspondent George Alagiah's forthright account of the growing intimacies between journalists and humanitarian agencies, the new relation of dependency is now firmly reciprocal: "[Humanitarian] agencies depend upon us for publicity and we need them to tell us where the stories are."[5]

This growing influence is, however, circumscribed in ways that frequently do more to *enhance* the hegemonic power of the West than to challenge it. As Kay Schaffer and Sidonie Smith argue, promoting accounts of human rights abuse "in print or through the media by and large depends upon a Western-based publishing industry, media, and readership." And this "dependence affects the kinds of stories published and circulated, the forms these stories take, and the appeals they make to audiences."[6] This untoward dependency affects the capacity of human rights NGOs to intervene in circuits of *international* visibility in terms of largely restricting such interventions to the representation of human rights abuses *outside* of Western Europe and North America. To the degree that human rights NGOs have tended to emphasize problems in non-Western countries, they have come to supply the discourse and practice of Western imperialism with a highly renewable source of alibis for intervention. Despite success in positioning themselves as key sources of information for international news, the capacity of human rights NGOs to substantially redraw the imaginary geographies of colonial modernity remains stymied by their relative inability to promote the recognition of human rights abuses inside Euro-America.

In response to this unwanted complicity, the tendency among human rights activists is to suppose that the persistent contradictions and hypocrisies of international recognition will be overcome through greater visibility and more public pressure. But what if the persistence of such obstacles also has something to do with the limits of a political practice predicated on the mobilization of shame? What if the discourse of shame actually provides ideological cover to the old Cold War calculus? What if shaming operations promote, however unwittingly and unintentionally, a *necessary* misrecognition of geopolitics and power that renders them largely ineffective as an anti-imperialist political form? These are the possibilities that I consider in closer detail in the remainder of this chapter.

In order to do this I examine two recent cinematic attempts to represent histories of catastrophic violence, Terry George's *Hotel Rwanda* (2004) and Michael Haneke's *Caché* (2005). There are a few reasons why I look to the cinema to examine the politics of shame and not, as might be expected, from within human rights practice. One is that in recent years NGO human rights organizations have found an important new ally in the circuits of mass market cinema. Consequently the effective visibility of a human rights frame is not confined to the production of human rights documents alone. I do not mean to suggest by this that films have simply taken up the role of promoting human rights, either through direct advocacy or willful propaganda. Rather, the influence of human rights discourse is beginning to be felt upon the cinematic narrative insofar as human rights has come to provide a unifying discursive framework for mapping (post-)colonial violence in the post–Cold War era. In other words, when contemporary filmmakers take up the subject of violence in the third world (or South), especially when produced for the first world (or North), the cultural scripts bear the traces of the growing ascendancy of human rights discourse. Correlatively, it is through the medium of the cinema with its international scope and popularity (and not, generally speaking, the human rights report) that audiences around the world increasingly learn about and see tragedies hitherto inaccessible and relatively invisible.[7] According to Allen Feldman, the influence of human rights upon our cultural imaginary includes playing a critical role in providing the stories of violence and abuse, prescribing a framework for witnessing (both testimonial and spectatorial), structuring the modes of intelligibility (largely through the psychoanalytic registers of trauma and healing), and overdetermining the moral message.[8]

Another set of reasons for looking at film pertains to the specific question of how *shame* operates within the discourse of human rights. In the practices that make up the bulk of human rights fieldwork, such as fact-finding, information gathering, documenting, publishing, and reporting, the actual ideological work of shame remains largely implicit — *behind* but not *in* the text, *behind* but not *in* the appeals to the Truth Commission, and so on. That is to say, within the pragmatic human rights text the question of shame, and who is to bear the brunt of shame, is largely given over to a determination and identification of guilty parties. Thus *responsibil-ity* and *accountability* constitute the visible or surface figures in the human rights text, as conditioned by the legal modes of representa-tion and as distinguished from the entertainment text of the cinema. In the case of both *Hotel Rwanda* and *Caché*, however, the shaming operation is itself made visible. In contrast to the relatively invis-ible machinations of shame in the legalistic discourse of the human rights text, the architectonics of shame are made constitutive of the narrative of violence in these films. Thus these films afford us a unique opportunity to examine the politics of shame as they shape the ethical practice of human rights and as this politic has come to participate in the (re)production of subjects for empire.

Hotel Rwanda, Who Is "We"?

The highly acclaimed film *Hotel Rwanda* (2004), directed by Terry George, is organized around the dilemmas and actions of two central characters, Paul Rusesabagina, the manager of the Belgian-owned Milles Collines Hotel in Kigali, and Colonel Oliver, the head United Nations peace-keeping official, ostensibly assigned to stop the genocidal violence in mid-1994.[9] It is not, strictly speaking, a story of the 1994 genocide in Rwanda. Rather, George wanted to recount the atrocity in Rwanda in such a way that it would, accord-ing to him, have broad cinematic appeal and, at the same time, elicit for the future what has come to be popularly known as "the lesson of Rwanda." In order to do this, George strategically reduced the enormity of the genocide largely to the difficulties faced by these two characters.[10] In the words of the director of *Hotel Rwanda,* this process took the following form:

> I was trying to write a film about Africa, about the political situation and the kind of...anarchy and hopelessness that ordinary people have to endure. And then I came across a first draft of Kier Pearson's version of this story. I realized that this was a human story that would allow me to tell this overwhelming political and humanitarian story, but tell it in a way that it could become a piece of entertainment as a movie, [and] make people laugh and cry and feel anger and sorrow and ultimately to feel uplifted that the ordinary man can triumph over evil.[11]

George's desire for a therapeutic resolution to contain what he refers to as the "horrific element of [the genocide]" and to "uplift" through the biographical story of Paul Rusesabagina was critically coupled with the shaming operations embodied in the figure of the United Nations official.[12] It is the interplay between these two figures that grounds, filters, and transmits the moral message in the screened consumption of the catastrophe.

The narrative and theatrical techniques deployed are critically directed toward the indifference of the West/North with respect to the genocide and the imperialist tendency toward historical amnesia when it comes to racialized violence.[13] The character of Paul Rusesabagina is figured as the heroic protagonist who deserves rescue, but does not receive it, while Colonel Oliver is the frustrated international official who bears the weight of shame brought about through the failure of international institutions to intercede on behalf of Paul Rusesabagina and the Rwandan people. The primary series of messages is rather poignantly directed: *we should have done something; nearly one million died while the world stood by and did nothing; we can never let this happen again.*

In its exclusive focus on the victim-hero and the failure of the West to intervene, *Hotel Rwanda* encodes the dense materiality of violent history into a master narrative of virtual witnessing that demands a break with the past toward an enlightened future yet to come. History is reduced to a traumatic historical event, singular and archaicized, to be consumed elsewhere as an entertaining injunction of "never again." Guided by an interest to make a popular film about the horrors of mass violence and communicate a moral and therapeutic message, George carefully avoids any potentially polluting exposure that the slaughter might have on viewers. As he says:

> I wanted to make a movie that everyone could go and see and not feel that they had to turn their heads away, that they would be caught up in the tension of it, they'd be caught up in the love story between this devoted husband and wife and also caught up in the human drama and feel that they are with Paul, so the horrific element, it was important for me not to focus on that at all; I didn't want anyone to feel that they could avoid this film because it was gory and it would be distasteful to them.[14]

The complex task of telling the story of the Rwandan genocide within the ideological and institutional constraints of the mass-market cinema was to be overcome with the transmutation of tragedy through a therapeutic screen and a transposition of the local and the particular onto the plane of the putatively universal. "Decontextualization," Allen Feldman suggests, "is the first movement in the universalization of the narrative of victimage."[15] Rather than diminishing the truth-effect of the account, however, the narrative finds ample ideological support in the universalization project of transnational human rights that has increasingly come to provide and/or condition the cultural scripts through which mass violence outside the West is viewed, read, and comprehended. Within the asymmetric theater of witnessing that reinforces the international division of justice, the transpositions appear seamless, allowing for the widest possible audience to receive the truth-effect of the narrative.

> This movie is supposed to tell the truth of what happened in Rwanda, so that what happened in our country might not happen anywhere else in the world. It is a good lesson. It is supposed to be a good lesson to the international community. For them, at least one day, if they face another situation they could say, "Let us not make the same mistakes as we did in Rwanda."[16]

While such sentiments have a great deal of immediate humanitarian appeal, their apparent simplicity betrays a much more complex and difficult set of questions: Who is this international community? Who is this "we" that should have done something? What should this "we" have done? What if this "we" were already doing a great deal in Rwanda? What if what "we" were doing in Rwanda was in fact a major contributing cause to the slaughter? And if this is the case, what becomes of the question: "What should we have done?" To raise these questions is to complicate what passes invariably as "the failure in Rwanda" or, what amounts to the same thing, the "lesson of Rwanda." And to consider that perhaps the lesson, or rather *lessons,* are not what we have come to suppose them to be.

The film is organized into four parts: the pregenocide moment, the beginning and early phases of the slaughter (up to the withdrawal of the West), the postwithdrawal strategies of survival, and the retreat to safety (and the reconciliation of the extended family of survivors). The middle two sections make up the overwhelming bulk of the film. For the better part of the first half of the film, the anticipation of an imminent rescue by the United Nations is held before us. Any day now, the emplotment suggests, the UN will arrive; until then, just buy time. And, literally, this is what Paul Rusesabagina, the shrewd manager, does; craftily using his connections and his wiles to protect all those in the hotel from the slaughter occurring just outside the hotel's gates. Then suddenly, as hope is beginning to fade, a caravan of white soldiers appears. More than in any other scene in the film, this is where the operations of cinematic shame will be most resoundingly affixed to Colonel Oliver, the UN, and the West.

It runs like this. As the caravan approaches, shouts ring out: "They're here! They're here!" Smiles of relief wash over the faces of the Rwandans and the foreigners trapped in the hotel. "The soldiers have arrived!" Images of handshakes and hugs abound. Warm greetings of "Welcome." Paul and Tatiana (Paul's wife) kiss. Then, suddenly, Paul begins to sense that all is not as it seems. Colonel Oliver is seen in the distance arguing with the soldier in command. Oliver throws his hat on the ground in apparent disgust. The smile fades from Paul's face. The colonel storms back into the hotel and takes a seat at the empty hotel bar. Paul follows, taking up his servant position behind the bar. With apparent obliviousness, Paul asks: "So, Colonel, what can I get for you?" The colonel orders a drink, sits quietly, head bowed. Paul, still unsure about what is happening, offers praise: "Congratulations, Colonel, you have performed a minor miracle." The colonel mutters incredulously, "Congratulations?" Paul, somewhat confused by the colonel's response, replies: "Yes, Sir." Brief dramatic pause. Looking up from his drink, the colonel pointedly declares: "You should spit in my face." Duly confused, Paul asks the colonel to repeat himself: "Excuse me, Colonel?" After another brief pause, the colonel continues with the following declaration: "You're dirt. . . . We think you're dirt, Paul." Paul with dawning recognition: "Who is *we?*" (without pause) the colonel replies, "The West, all the superpowers, everything you believe in, Paul, they think you're dirt, they think you're dung, you're worthless!" Paul, refusing to believe what he is hearing, but still with steadfast politeness, persists: "I'm afraid I don't understand what you're saying, Sir?" The colonel, interrupting, spells it out: "Oh, c'mon, don't bullshit me, Paul, you're the smartest man here, you've got 'em eating out of your hands, hell, you could own this freakin' hotel except for one thing: you're BLACK!" After a brief pause, the colonel continues: "You're not even a nigger; you're an African. . . . They're not gonna stay, Paul. They're not gonna stop the slaughter." The scene ends. Despite the injunction to do so, Paul does not spit in the colonel's face. A short while later, all the non-Rwandans are evacuated.[17]

The transmutation of the genocide in Rwanda into the lesson of Rwanda is the emplotted product of the twin operations through which the global mission of international human rights is secured, reanimated, and sanctified. That this global mission lands squarely on the shoulders of the imperialist West, with its more-than-dubious record of "humanitarian intervention," passes unremarked in the triumphal spirit of the ordinary man:

> There are two things that I hope [people] will take [from the film]. First of all, that if they dig deep down within themselves and into their moral center . . . there's great courage and hope and charity amongst all of us to overcome any evil. I think that's the fundamental story of Paul, the greatness of the human spirit. The second thing is that in the wider political story of Rwanda human beings are a more important element, a more important commodity to the world, than oil or gold or silver or platinum or diamonds. And when we start realizing that it's worthwhile to go in and rescue people . . . to stop these sorts of humanitarian crises going on, then I think the world will be a much better place.[18]

The failure to intervene is registered as the product of a retrograde racist ideology, but there is no corresponding recognition that either the mode of appeal *to* the West, or the desired intervention *from* the West, constitute any sort of imperialist ethos worth questioning. The fact that the entire question of agency resides *in the West* and *with the West* is elided in the narrative mobilization of shame. This is not to suggest that the actions and inactions of powerful nation-states in the West/North did not act shamefully, but to recognize that the way the moral question is structured insists on the centrality of Western Man as the guarantor and protector of rights and humanity. The hero functions only to underscore what the West should have done, why we should have intervened. Such a humanist plea for intervention erases the active presence of the West in Rwanda prior to and during the genocide. That is to say, in the process of making the genocide *visible* the script of shame renders the active role of the West, through long and continuing histories of colonial and postcolonial exploitation and violence, largely *invisible*.

Such a critique should call into question the racial politics of the film; instead George has been lauded for casting a black man as the protagonist in *Hotel Rwanda*.[19] Despite such praise, it is important to recognize that the construction of the victim-hero in this context is predicated upon figuring an individual who is palatable to the West. In order to function as a deserving victim-hero,

Rusesabagina's racial difference must be domesticated. In this case, Rusesabagina's domesticated worthiness emanates from his role as hotel manager in an elite colonial hotel. Rusesabagina's labor involves pampering local elites and Western tourist and business classes, and he is depicted as performing this task earnestly and without any resentment or disdain for those whom he serves. He is accommodating and pleasant throughout, granting all requests with a smile and a "thank you, sir." He performs his labor in the service of the global economy without ideology, avoiding any hint of entitlement or critical agency. Paul has the perfect disposition, a totally passive postcolonial subject with respect to his exploitation. His wife, Tatiana, is the perfect sexist complement to him, reduced as she is to performing the role of the dutiful wife, faithfully clinging to her husband's heroics. A family like the Rusesabagina's, the narrative wants to say, deserves our rescue. Thus *Hotel Rwanda* recognizes that racism plays a critical role in the indifference of the West, and it challenges such indifference by offering up the eminently likeable couple of Paul and Tatiana with children. In this way the semiotic inclusion of racial others is carefully evacuated of any undomesticated difference — no critical voice, no agency, nothing but the desire to serve the postcolonial tourist economy, make money, and raise a family in peace. It is in this way that Paul becomes the perfect character to transmit the lesson of Rwanda despite his racial otherness, as his character passes through the domesticating frame of postcolonial passivity and subservience. The potentially "disturbing" or "disrupting" fact of blackness and Africanness (racial and geographic difference), which might otherwise disqualify Paul and the Rwandan people from meritorious victimhood, is neutralized in the apparent willingness to faithfully accept the position of subordination in the global economy.

The lesson is clear: to qualify for recognition as a *deserving* victim, the colonized subject must adopt a pose of absolute passivity with respect to the labor extraction schemes of the West. The narrative rigorously mutes any critical agency or voice from the victims of genocide as it strictly circuits the representation of violence through the heroics of the deserving victim, the domesticated other. The deserving victim cannot take up arms or be an advocate of anything other than the desire to survive and, in this case, save his family and other innocent victims. Innocence and the willingness to accept racist structures of exploitation have become the prerequisites for qualifying as a victim across the international division of humanity. Quite contradictorily, however, the rescue occurs when Paul and the hotel guests are able to drive to safety behind the protected lines of the armed Tutsi resistance fighters. But this actual moment of rescue passes completely unremarked in "the story which tells itself" insofar as no subjects of resistance are allowed visibility within the cathartic frame of individual heroism and international failure. Apparently such stories have no place in a discourse carefully expunged of any plurality or collectivity, save for those of the clearly deserving victim.

The representation of persons in need of rescue is by no means innocent, even when the subjects represented may rightfully be considered so. Humanitarian intervention, or the depoliticization of military intervention, has come to rely upon images of domesticated alterity (ideals of domesticity) in which the realities of historical depth and complexity are sacrificed on the altar of a globalizing mission whose amnesias have come to serve as an infinitely renewable source of alibis for post–Cold War imperialist interventionism. The political imperative of making visible within which the film wants to operate is achieved at the cost of continually reanimating the ideological structures of legitimation that provide a convenient cover for the interventionary designs of the new imperialism.[20]

In his classic ethnography *Shamanism, Colonialism, and the Wildman*, Michael Taussig argues that the postcolonial curative project is entangled with a complicity in historical violence that remains tacit but unacknowledged.[21] In the shaming operations of George's version of traumatic realism, history becomes epistemologically grounded in the ahistorical. The position of the shamed is figured as exterior to the site(s) of violence from which the presumption of failure to intervene can be lodged and from which the demand for intervention is called forth. But if the relation of the West to racialized colonial and postcolonial violence is not one of exteriority, but always already inside, then the trope of shame is a performative ruse behind which the imbrication of the West in the postcolony, as much as in the colony, continues to hide with relative impunity. What George carefully expunges from the text of the moral-therapeutic narrative are the contradictory traces that reveal that "the we who should have done something" are already involved in the production and reproduction of postcolonial violence. As Feldman concludes in his account of the trauma-aesthetic:

It is no coincidence that recent post-9/11 discourses on barbarism/ civilization have justified military interventions on the other side of the world as humanitarian aid, and that humanitarian aid itself has been militarized and transformed into a mode of policing. In many instances the mediatization of witnessing through commissions of inquiry or electronic circulation is but the creation, replication, and enforcement of such difference, marking virtual boundaries in a world rife with political complicity, leaky ideological borders, and interspatial accountability.[22]

In the next section I want to examine one possible cinematic rejoinder to the modernist ethos of *Hotel Rwanda*. Within the discourses of postmodern visual culture, the realist aesthetics of George have long been out of fashion and a more deconstruction-ist approach preferred. In the postmodern text the insistence is on self-reflexivity, and when such practices are tethered to a political critique, the injunction is to undermine existing representational practices from within. While such practices may have a certain critical force in exposing, among other things, the contradictions of modernist historiography, they tend to encounter their own set of limits when approaching the histories of racialized, colonial, and postcolonial violence. In one of the more interesting recent cine-matic attempts to represent colonial violence in a postmodern mode, we will turn now to consider Michael Haneke's *Caché*. I will not provide an extensive analysis of the film; rather I discuss it here briefly in order to see how the kind of postmodern critique that Haneke's film advances over and against the realism of George and *Hotel Rwanda* also suffers from the strict limits of an imperial gaze that is systematically unable to approach the question of violence so elaborately theorized by Fanon some fifty years earlier.

Caché and the Postcolonial Optics of Disavowal

The historical anchor for Michael Haneke's fictional film *Caché* involves the massacre of two hundred Algerians during a demon-stration in Paris in 1961. According to Haneke, the slaughter was brought to his attention when he happened by chance upon a documentary broadcast on French television. Haneke was "totally shocked that [he] had never heard of this event before."[23] The "silence" surrounding this event not only spanned some forty years, but also encompassed the highly public 1998 trial of the man at the center of the slaughter, Maurice Papon. In his trial Papon was convicted of "crimes against humanity" for his role in sending more than sixteen hundred Jewish people to their deaths during World War II. Although Papon was not on trial for his involvement with the murders in 1961 (during which time he was serving as Paris chief of police), stories of his notorious history came to light as a result of publicity surrounding the trial. Prior to his belated fall from grace, Papon had a distinguished and highly decorated career of civil service. In 1942 he was appointed general-secretary of the prefecture of Gironde, under the collaborationist Vichy government. It was during his tenure as prefecture that he ordered the deportation of thousands of Jews to detention camps in Bordeaux. Most went on to the concentration camp at Auschwitz, and all but a few were murdered. He held his post until late 1944. In mid-1944, when it was clear that the war was turning against the Germans, Papon began to inform on the Nazis to the resistance — actions for which he was later decorated with the coveted Carte d'Ancien Combattant de la Resistance. From 1947 to 1949 the celebrated bureaucrat was appointed to the post of the préfet in the colonial territories of Corsica and Algeria, and from 1958 to 1968 he served as chief of the Paris police under de Gaulle. In 1970 he turned to elected politics and became a cabinet minister in the French parliament, ultimately ascending to the appointment of budget minister in 1978 under President Valery Giscard D'Estaing. In 1981, however, Papon's past came back to haunt him.

The Papon affair, as it would come to be known in France, began in earnest in 1981, when hundreds of documents were found in the recesses of the Bordeaux town hall. Among the papers discovered were a large number of deportation orders signed by Papon. He would eventually stand trial for this discovery some fifteen years later. Throughout the trial, Papon was resolute in proclaiming his innocence, preferring to cast himself as a savior of the Jews. He told the court that he kept his job to try to help the Resistance and conduct an underground struggle to help Jews. He also maintained that he did not know what was happening to those that he put on the trains. On more than one occasion he asked the court, "What should one have done?" In the end, Papon was found guilty for crimes against humanity but escaped with a not guilty charge for complicity in the murder of the sixteen hundred deportees. As mentioned above, however, Papon's high-level role in the genocide of Jewish persons during the occupation was not his only involvement with mass murder, even though it was the only case for which he was tried. During his tenure as head of the Paris police (1958–68) Papon's murderous law-and-orderism took aim at a large group of Algerian protestors in Paris in October 1961. At a critical juncture in anticolonial resistance to the French occupation of Algeria, Algerians living in Paris took to the streets demanding an end to colonial rule in their native country. Chief Papon ordered a crackdown that resulted in the murder of at least two hundred Algerians. The dead bodies were summarily dumped into the Seine River. This slaughter was concealed from the public for years as journalists were censored, the official death toll hushed, and French political elites closed ranks around the Algerian question.

In Haneke's fictional rendition of these historic events, the Austrian filmmaker opts not to restage the collective resistance of the Algerian people (as in *Battle of Algiers*)[24] or their collective massacre in the streets of Paris on October 17, 1961 (as in *Drowning by Bullets*).[25] Instead Haneke's postmodern narrative uses a different kind of countering strategy to record the legacies of colonial violence. As Haneke suggests, "the question isn't 'how do I show violence?' but rather 'how do I show the spectator his position vis-à-vis violence and its representation?' "[26] And in keeping with this directive, Haneke lodges a critique of the West by situating the Western bourgeois subject in relation to the history of racialized violence. In *Caché*, Haneke dramatizes the difficulties involved in breaking through the ideological screens behind which the contemporary bourgeoisie hide to avoid (historic) responsibility. Haneke appears to want to compel an engagement with the historical in order to address the question of the relationship between the colonial past (and its racialized violence) and the neocolonial present (marked by willful forgetting), in order to signal the possibilities for a postcolonial future. The mediatized environment is demonstrably visible in every shot of the film, from the surveillance camera to the bookshelves that line the (intellectual) bourgeois home to the television show that Georges Laurent hosts. And yet, despite the overwhelming presence of the postmodern visible (or perhaps because of it), much remains invisible. In order to get to the bourgeois subject, to compel self-reflection and historical recognition, the mediated spectacles that lay claim to (or are pawned off as) the representation of the real, must be interrupted.

The opening salvo in Haneke's critical take on the active blindness of the metropolitan bourgeoisie is carried out through an excessive play of visual technologies — multiple cameras, a television screen, videotapes, and a video recorder. The film begins with a long shot from a static camera of the outside of a home on a relatively quiet street in a middle-class Parisian neighborhood. Credits role across the screen in teletype fashion. There is no musical accompaniment to adulterate the optical (either in this opening scene or throughout the movie); instead we hear only the sounds of a natural early morning street scene — birds chirping, a car door shutting, indistinct ambient noise. Minutes pass. A male voice is heard over the image: "Well?" A female voice responds: "Nothing." Still shot persists. Male voice: "Where was it?" Female voice: "In a plastic bag on the porch.... What's wrong?" Cut. Fixed shot, same residence, different angle. Man comes out of doorway, followed by a woman. As he proceeds to cross the street, a mobile camera follows. He walks toward the location where he believes the camera would have been located, shouts to the woman: "He must have been there, no?" Somewhat apprehensive, the woman responds: "Come inside." Cut. Return to a fixed shot of the outside of the house. Voiceover conversation renews. Suddenly, the image begins to rewind. At this point, we realize that the couple, and we the viewers, are watching a videotaped image. Woman's voice: "The tape runs for over two hours." Image continues to rewind. "There." Rewind is stopped. Fast forward. Rewind. Stop. The man is seen walking into the shot, presumably walking right by the still camera. Man: "How come I didn't see him? It'll remain a mystery." Tape rolls on, nothing much happening save for random street comings and goings. Cut. The man and the woman are in their living room watching the videotape on the television. He shuts off the TV. Both shake their heads. Man: "It's dumb. I don't know what to say." Man shuts off the videorecorder. The couple offers mildly curious speculation as to who might be behind the mystery. The following day, after a short scene at their son's swimming practice, the fixed camera shot returns. A second recording, same shot as the first, only now it is night time. Through this opening play of visual fields, Haneke has established the spectre of a continuously running recording device poised to capture everything that happens, from the banal quotidian to, as we shall see, the violent historical.

The intrusion of the all-seeing recording device into the home via the videotape disturbs the placid comforts of the metropolitan bourgeoisie. The disturbance is effected through a blurring and destabilization of the spatial distinction between the private and the public. The "right to individual privacy" is herein figured as a critical means by which the bourgeoisie shelter themselves, as we shall see, from historic shame. In an important critical maneuver, Haneke constructs a sequencing of events which imply that it is the destabilization of the public-private binary that allows for the possibility for a historical reckoning to take place — without this partial undoing, the narrative implies, no engagement is possible. The upsetting intrusions proliferate in the form of more tapes (six in all) and a series of postcards sent to the Laurent's home, to the Laurent's child at school, to Georges at work, and ultimately to Georges's boss at work. Many of the subsequent communicative acts are accompanied by a child's drawing highlighting a bloody incident. Each successive intrusion ("terrorist acts" in Georges Laurent's terms) provides more clues for Georges as to the agent behind the mystery, insofar as he comes to recognize the past events that he is being forced to recollect.

Despite Georges reluctance to share his increasing knowledge of the meaning of the cryptic messages with anyone else, even his wife, who is reasonably traumatized by them, he is ultimately compelled to divulge their historic significance. It is here that we learn that following the 1961 massacre of Algerians in Paris, Georges's parents were set to adopt an Algerian boy, Majid, whose parents were among those killed. The young Georges, however, did not like the prospect of sharing the bourgeois comforts of his childhood with the other boy, and so he concocted a story of the boy's affliction with tuberculosis — a racist trope with a rich history in the annals of imperial violence against the colonized. The plot worked and Georges's parents had the boy sent away to an orphanage. Georges never thought about the boy again, until the forced reengagement via the mysterious videotapes in the postcolonial present. Despite his actions, his lies (past and present), and his attempted cover up, Georges insists that he bears no contemporary responsibility: "I was just a child."

The unsavory reckoning with the past reaches the point where Georges comes to confront Majid, who is currently living in poverty in an Algerian neighborhood in Paris. Majid insists he is not the agent behind the camera. Despite Georges's accusations and despite the great lengths to which Georges has reluctantly been brought to confront his past and its living and dead weight upon the present, his ability to deflect any hint of shame or responsibility is the point of Haneke's relentless assault on the comfortable family life of the contemporary metropolitan bourgeoisie. The critique of white, metropolitan amnesia is devastating, and Haneke's film rightly deserves credit for its assault on the Western Subject of indifference and colonial disavowal. The limit of his postmodern critical project is realized, however, at the point where the filmmaker might be said to merge with his protagonist.

In the film's most dramatic scene we begin to witness the effects of colonial violence from the other side. When Georges is brought to Majid's apartment, Majid appears to bear no great ill will toward him. He is gracious, kind, even appearing somewhat happy to see Georges after all these years. Majid sits passively in his one-room apartment, taking in Georges's accusations with requisite confusion (after all he doesn't know anything about the tapes). Majid does not appear to want anything from Georges in the way of an apology or anything else, but when met with accusations and threats, his only recourse is to weep — a response that we witness through the all-seeing eye of the historical recording device, the stationary camera. A short time later Majid summons Georges back to his apartment. Georges arrives. Majid thanks him for coming, invites him in, and asks him to sit down. Georges refuses, demanding to know what this is about. Majid reiterates that "he had no idea about the tapes." Georges in a highly perturbed state asks: "Is that all?" Majid calmly responds: "I called you because I wanted you to be present." Then, in a split second, Majid pulls out a razor and slashes his own throat. In this dramatic scene, Georges is made to witness the central defiant act of the colonized other in Haneke's fictional account: *suicide*. While this tragic act of self-immolatory violence is intended to underscore the ethical bankruptcy of white historical amnesia and disavowal of colonial violence in the cinematic text, it also points to the severe limits within which the Western liberal imaginary is bound up vis-à-vis the colonized other.

While a mounting sense of shame threatens to disturb Georges's increasingly uncomfortable existence (in the form of haunting, sweat-inducing dreams), sleeping pills and heavy curtains suffice to refract the consequences of both colonial and postcolonial instances of violence from his waking conscience. At this point, it is Majid's son who steps forth to confront Georges. The son appears at Georges's workplace. Despite the more assertive act of coming to his place of work, it is unclear what the young man wants. Georges moves them into the restroom and away from the front door to his office.[27] He interrogates the young man: "What do you want?" No response. Georges, reiterating more forcefully: "Young man, your father's death must hurt, but I refuse to be incriminated by you." With growing impatience, he asks again: "What do you want? A fight?" Placidly, the young man responds: "If you insist." Again Georges asserts his disavowal of responsibility: "I can tell you this, you'll never give me a bad conscience about your father's sad and wrecked life....I'm not to blame! Do you get that?...Do you expect me to apologize?" Majid's son in stoical fashion: "To who?" Georges incredulously: "So what do you want?" Majid's son responds: "Nothing anymore. I wondered how it feels, a man's life on your conscience. That's all. Now I know." Georges perturbed but with a hint of relief: "Great, everything's ok then. Do you mind if I go now?" Majid's son replies, impassively and with remarkable politesse: "Be my guest." Georges exits the bathroom. While the passivity of the colonial other in this scene serves to underscore the aggressivity of the colonizer, as well as the *mauvaise foi* within which such aggressivity and mechanisms of disavowal are couched, the limits of such an anticolonial critique can be gleaned in the sheer absence of any speaking back or acting against. All Majid's son appears to want in Haneke's text, despite the life and death of his father for which Georges is overwhelmingly responsible, is to witness Georges's (lack of) conscience!

In Haneke's *Caché*, then, it appears that both the colonial and postcolonial racial other is caught between suicide and nothing, while the white, bourgeois subject fends off any return of the colonial repressed. The purchase of ethical superiority on the part of the colonized comes with the high cost of passive victimhood and ineffectual innocence. This type of figure has become de rigueur in the cinematic text of Western, postcolonial shame (*pace Hotel Rwanda*), and while such a rendering portends to serve as a welcome advance over more explicitly racist accounts of colonial Others, its critical limits are palpably evident in its imaginary management of "political awareness into privatized emotional response."[28] The ethical elevation of the colonized is predicated on an evisceration of any substantial agency beyond the servility of "thank you, sir" and "be my guest." So while the echo of colonial violence is profound in *Caché*, the prescribed forms of opposition to racialized violence from the other side are meticulously contained within the regulatory structures of victimhood and domesticated otherness —

unthreatening, servile, deserving of sentimental attachment and rescue. In this way, despite his damning critique of Western Man,
Haneke appears incapable of moving beyond the moment of colonial paralysis (now in postcolonial guise) in which the racial Other is
given over to the dictates of nonviolence. Any political vision articulated through the (therapeutic) modality of shame or *mauvaise
foi*, however critical in intent, will necessarily remain incapable of
grasping the dialectical nature of colonial violence or of producing the ideological decentering of the (Subject of the) West which
it seeks.

In a rather sterile (but cinematically fascinating) attempt to signal an outside (or a beyond) to the colonial impasse into which the
narrative has drawn us, Haneke offers us a closing shot that revels
in its own ambiguity. The scene: a long-distance still shot of the
entrance to Pierrot's school, children with backpacks coming and
going. Seconds pass. Children continue to come and go. At some
point, a point often missed by viewers upon a first viewing the film,
Pierrot can be seen, to the left side of the screen, descending the
stairs. Once he reaches the bottom of the stairs, in the lower left
corner of the screen, he can be seen talking with Majid's son, who
has come to meet him in what appears as a planned encounter. They
chat for a minute in an amicable fashion and then separate. Fixed
shot is held; credits role. A plotting? A conspiracy? A sign of hope
for a new postcolonial future? Perhaps. Impute to the scene what
you will; it is open-ended. In terms of the mystery text, the who-
dunit, the shot helps to disrupt any lingering notions that Majid's
son might be or might have been the eye-behind-the-camera. And
given that he is the only remaining character who has been impli-
cated as the possible agent behind the recording device, the closing
shot helps to trouble any attempt to assign a human agent to the
workings of the still camera (hence providing more warrant for
reading the second camera as the recording of history itself).

The calculated indeterminacy of the scene is offered up as a sign
of a possible exteriority, a way out, and yet it is completely devoid
of any significance, political or otherwise, a hollow gesture toward
a future that will necessarily(?) be different. (After all it is not a confrontation, but a meeting; and there are no signs of antagonism, only
communication.) A postcolonial generation in the making? Again,
perhaps. All well and good, one supposes, but embarrassingly random, a sign that can only be taken for wonder and filled to the
brim with whatever significance one so chooses or simply left as an

empty signifier — a sort of promissory note for some political good to be delivered at some indeterminate time in some uncertain future ("justice yet to come," as they say). Clever but hollow, a homage to the best politics that deconstruction has to offer. We know for certain that the colonial bourgeoisie, in the form of Georges, will never get it, but there is hope for future generations, who appear to have begun to make a break from the past.

In contrast to *Hotel Rwanda,* the critical act of shaming the colonial bourgeoisie is all that we are left with in *Caché.* Haneke does not direct us anywhere and is instead content to leave us with a non-resolution full of ambiguity and undecidability. A totally pleasurable cinematic experience, but politically rather wanting. Contra *Caché, Hotel Rwanda* goes unabashedly for a liberal humanist resolution, wherein shame is directed toward mobilization. ("Let us not make the same mistakes as we did in Rwanda.") *Hotel Rwanda,* then, works to prepare us via the lesson of Rwanda toward a future where we will demand action, a future, that is, of humanitarian intervention.

Imperialism in the Foreseeable Future

It is a rather ironic fact of history that in times of extreme catastrophe — genocide, famine, natural disasters, etc. — calls abound from various quarters in the West for Western powers to intervene, to help in the name of humanity.[29] And what was once discussed as a question of "the right of intervention" has increasingly become, at least since 1948 and especially in the post–Cold War period, figured as our *duty* to intervene. And yet any sober account of this period, and not only this period, must reckon with the salient fact that the long history of Western intervention throughout the world, intervention of an unprecedented scope and scale, has resulted in the destruction of hundreds of millions of lives by slaughter, hunger, disease, and poverty. Despite such a dubious record in actual practice however, there remains a stubborn and persistent faith in the value and the duty of the West (and particularly its formerly foremost power, the United States) to intervene. This shift from the right of intervention to the duty to intervene is of profound importance. The former (the right of intervention) is a decidedly political question — subject to the potentially limiting conditions of sovereignty — while the latter (the duty to intervene) transposes the question of intervention onto a decontextualized, ahistorical moral terrain — no longer subject to any limiting conditions, reduced in form to the universal question of good versus evil, humanity versus inhumanity. This new universality taken out of the political realm and recast onto a moral plane makes it increasingly difficult to challenge the very question of intervention. This is constitutive, I believe, of what Edward Said once figured as a more general difficulty that we confront when attempting to critically deploy the discourse of human rights: "So completely has the power of the United States — under which in some measure we all live — invested even the vocabulary of universality that the search for 'new ideological means' to challenge it has become in fact more difficult."[30]

The shift from the right of intervention to the duty to intervene, with all the attendant paradoxes, has been facilitated in the post–Cold War era by a number of factors, including the hegemonic ascendancy of the discourse of human rights. As an increasingly critical legitimizing instrument for contemporary imperialism, human rights, and its imperial modes of intervention — humanitarian war and humanitarian aid — relies heavily upon the production of subjects in need — in need of rights, in need of democracy, in need of rescue. This subject-in-need, in turn, interpellates, organizes, and mobilizes subjects who come to see themselves as bearers of the responsibility to rescue — good humanitarians who, however critical of imperialism, come to participate in the ethos of Empire.

And while the films *Hotel Rwanda* and *Caché* dramatize the pervasive influence that a human rights episteme has come to have on the contemporary liberal-imperialist ethos via the machinations of shame, the Rwandan genocide in particular has come to play a critical role as the exemplary case of *the failure to intervene* in contemporary U.S. international relations theory — the political corollary to the popular culturalization of the lesson of Rwanda. Within international relations discourse, Rwanda is the standard bearer for this failure, while the NATO intervention of 1999 in Bosnia is held forth as the supposedly "successful case of humanitarian intervention."[31] In the annals of contemporary international relations discourse, the work of Samantha Power stands out as one of the most ambitious attempts to theorize the place of Rwanda within a long history of the U.S. failure to intervene in twentieth-century genocides.[32] In her Pulitzer prize–winning account, *A Problem from Hell: America and the Age of Genocide* (2002), Power purports to delineate a "pattern of nonintervention" on the part of U.S. administrations stretching from the Armenian genocide of 1915 to the Rwandan genocide of 1994. In the book Power tries to establish this "pattern of nonintervention" in order to advance her call for greater U.S. intervention in any future genocides, for a greater moral and political commitment to preventing and stopping genocide. She examines the cases of Armenian genocide of 1915, Pol Pot's reign of terror in Cambodia (1975–79), the mass killing of the Kurds in Iraq (1987–88), the Hutu slaughter of the Tutsi peoples of Rwanda, and the killings carried out by the Serbs, 1995–99 (she makes no mention of slaughters undertaken by Bosnian Muslims or Croats). This highly selective history and analysis of twentieth-century genocides ignores the mass slaughters in Hiroshima and Nagasaki, East Timor, and Guatemala, as well as those in Vietnam, Palestine, and Colombia, to name but a few. In all these cases the role of the United States was far from that of nonintervention.

If we attend to the full historical record of U.S. interventions, it becomes clear that the role of the United States with respect to genocide includes all of the following forms of activity:

1. precipitating, participating in, and helping carry out genocide

2. acting in such ways as to escalate genocide

3. blocking attempts to mitigate genocide

4. doing nothing

5. facilitating attempts to mitigate genocide

Of these forms of involvement, only the action of "doing nothing" can rightfully be considered as a form of *nonintervention* and on that account only the Armenian genocide of 1915 might qualify. In all the other cases, one or more of the other categories of activity applies. In the case of Rwanda, for example, Clinton refused Belgium's request to reinforce the UN peacekeeping mission prior to and during the early days of slaughter and less than a week into the killings insisted that all UN peacekeepers withdraw from the country. And all such actions by the United States were undertaken while denying that genocide was taking place. In other words, to try to extract a pattern of U.S. nonintervention with respect to twentieth-century genocides is baleful at best. There simply is no pattern. There are instead a series of strategic actions and tactical responses guided by an imperial calculus of elite–national interest.

In light of the actual historical record, we might be inclined to write off Power's account as simply bad historiography that happened to win a Pulitzer prize, but we need to recognize that this bad historiography has a history and is more or less the official account that Washington elites like to tell themselves and the rest of us. Central to this ideological enterprise is the scripting of Washington as an outsider to such horrors, an exterior power watching from afar. This is a patently false act of historical revisionism that is nonetheless absolutely critical if one wants to advance an argument for greater levels of U.S. intervention in the future. In Power's account it is what allows her in the book's final pages to raise the specter of an urgent critical question: "Why does the US stand idly by?"[33]

Indeed it is upon this false narrative of a grim record of nonintervention that she makes her appeal for more and more intervention, as she writes: "For the foreseeable future, it will be up to the US to take the lead in stopping and punishing genocide."[34] And again, "American leadership will be indispensable in assembling coalitions of the willing to deploy ground troops, [and] in encouraging US allies to step up their capacities."[35] Clearly there is a problem with calling on Washington to take the lead in fighting something it has helped perpetuate on numerous occasions and carried out itself in a number of others. Her appeal to the American political establishment on the basis of morality and enlightened self-interest (genocides create instability) is horribly ill conceived. In contrast to Power's contention that we must look, "for the foreseeable future" to the United States for world leadership on preventing genocide and punishing those responsible, I would suggest that the foreseeable future actually has fairly predictable coordinates that we can identify in anticipating what role the United States is likely to play in twenty-first-century genocides. The hegemonic strategy of the United States, in the face of an imminent decline of its political and economic superiority, involves the pursuit of nothing less than to establish Washington's military control over the entire planet.

Elite opinion in the United States is decisively and uniformly in the corner of aggressively pursuing global military dominance. As Samir Amin says, "The ruling class of the United States freely proclaims that it will not 'tolerate' the reconstitution of any economic or military power capable of challenging its global domination. To this end, it has given itself the right to wage 'preventive wars.' "[36]

Prevailing elite opinion has determined, certainly for the foreseeable future, that U.S. military power is the only means of trying to sustain its existing economic advantages. In point of fact the United States has no decisive economic advantages in the current global economy. As Amin suggests, without military dominance, "the US would probably not be able to compete with Europe or Japan in high technology, with China, Korea and other industrial countries of Asia or Latin America in ordinary manufacturing products, or with Europe or the Southern Cone of Latin America in agriculture."[37] It is out of this context that an elite consensus has emerged that assumes that increasing our military superiority is our only means of warding off a fully multipolar world. With six thousand military bases at home and in its territories, and another eight hundred-plus owned or leased in over 130 countries around the world, the U.S. imperial project of pursuing global military dominance seems crystal clear. Such militaristic ambitions have come to constitute the strategic center of contemporary U.S. imperialism, as Chalmers Johnson recently suggested: "Once upon a time you could trace the spread of imperialism by counting up colonies. America's version of the colony is the military base."[38]

There is in fact no reason to suppose, as Power does, that if only America would take up its moral duty to intervene in cases of genocide that the world would be all the better for it. The historical record of U.S. interventions simply cannot sustain this assumption. And there is even less reason to suppose that things would be better still if the Pentagon were to act preemptively against "potential" genocide (another position she advocates), acquiring yet another pretext for its imperial mission. In the context of accelerated and unprecedented U.S. military expansion around the globe, Power's book is dangerously wrong and dangerously wrong-headed, and yet liberal commentators fawned over it. Hell, it sounded good: a critique of the U.S. political establishment for ignoring inhuman levels of slaughter and a forceful plea to elevate morality over politics in U.S. foreign policy. Who wouldn't agree to that?

As I've tried to show in this chapter, the conditions of possibility for such an uncritical reception may have something to do with the peculiar ways in which human rights discourse has come to condition the ways in which political violence outside the West is viewed and understood. A form of ideological conditioning that reinforces the constitution of subjects for Empire under the guise of anti-imperialist critique. Central to such operations are the privileging of rescue over solidarity in the production of humanitarian sensibilities that cannot help but approach the world except from the position of "but we have to do something!" The impoverished reduction of our political imaginary to that of saving subject, however well-meaning and good intentioned, will never allow us to develop the "new ideological means" necessary to challenge our imperialist ethos. For that I think we need to take seriously what the overwhelming majority of the South knows: Western humanitarian intervention is guided by a brute calculus of power, and no amount of mosquito nets or aid workers will ever cover over this fact.

4

Expiation for the Dispossessed

Truth Commissions, Testimonios, and Tyrannicide

> Among all the forms of violence permitted by both natural law and positive law there is not one that is free of the gravely problematic nature ... of all legal violence. Since, however, every conceivable solution to human problems, not to speak of deliverance from the confines of all the world-historical conditions of existence obtaining hitherto, remains impossible if violence is totally excluded in principle, the question necessarily arises as to other kinds of violence than all those envisaged by legal theory.
> — Walter Benjamin, "Critique of Violence"

Law, Terror, Truth

In his 1996 Wellek Lectures at the University of California at Irvine, French philosopher Étienne Balibar argued that "history is the means by which violence is converted into nonviolence and is transferred into political institutions."[1] One of the benefits of this formulation is to foreground the importance of representation as a critical mechanism by which violence is preserved and reproduced in the structure of state institutions.[2] History is more than simply a supplement to the explicitly repressive state apparatuses (the army, the police, prisons, and the judicial system); it is part and parcel of "the code of organized public violence" that regulates the field of legitimate (law) and illegitimate (terror) uses of violence.[3] When the "illusory opposition between Law and Terror"[4] suffers a fundamental breakdown and can no longer be reproduced through the routinized and normalized operations of hegemony, the legitimacy of the state must be reconstituted (such as following periods

of extreme violence — apartheid, dictatorship, fascism, totalitari-
anism). Under such conditions of radical crisis, the historiographic
function takes center stage.

The hegemonic task that stands before History in such periods
of crisis is to provide a passage from a past to a future whose
possibility of continuity has been rendered discontinuous through
the failure of the state to maintain the necessary fictions of Law.
This is a moment of great conjunctural opportunity in which the
convertibility of violence, or its fundamental nonconvertibility, is
collectively called into question. What gets rehabilitated in the wake
of such "exceptional moments" is deeply uncertain, up-for-grabs. So
while the state is occupied with the conversion of violence into nonviolence, counterhegemonic cultural productions labor to produce
signs of nonconvertibility.

In recent decades, in the aftermath of conditions of "extreme violence," a new institutional form has been designed to negotiate the
relation between past and present: the Truth Commission. Whether
this institution can serve to ideologically rehabilitate the state or
function as a repository for the critical tensions that have brought
the force of law to its threshold (or perhaps both at the same time),
remains a somewhat open-ended question. What can be said, for
certain, is that Truth Commissions have become one of the most
important institutional forms yet devised to advance the project
of human rights into the twenty-first century. They have emerged
in contexts of extreme violence as the preferred official modality
charged with the complex task of attempting to document and
redress past acts of collective violence, with more than thirty established in the last two decades. To this end, Truth Commissions have
been set up as transit mechanisms between the past and the future,
under what advocates call "the movement from repressive regimes
to democratic societies."[5] But how does the Truth Commission pur-
port to work? What kind of work does it do? What is its target? Its
aims? Its goals? Its techniques? What kind of public/official archive
does it produce? What is the nature of its "Truth"? And how does
the production of such a truth contribute to what is commonly figured as the goal of the commission: reconciliation? And if that is an
aim of the Truth Commission form, just how do we get from the
trauma archives of the past to the reconciled future? How does a
Truth Commission, of whatever specific design, set to work upon
a past of extreme violence in order to help secure a future state of

nonviolence? In sum, how does the Truth Commission attempt to convert violence into nonviolence?

Advocates for Truth Commissions suggest that this mode of transitional justice offers a new form of judicialism distinct from traditional institutions of Law, insofar as the Truth Commission functions less like a punishment machine than as a recording apparatus, by putting a record of past violence in an official archive. Such an archival project, it is hoped, will work against historical amnesia/disavowal and will begin to lay the foundations for a future public morality. But perhaps more important than producing a documentary record, it is in the process of production that the Truth Commission offers its most distinctive aspect: *therapeusis*. As a therapeutic apparatus, the process of producing the truth affords the voice of the victim a central place, insofar as the primary modality of conversion is attempted via the facilitation of testimony.[6] In this restorative forum victims are provided an institutional stage in which their accounts will be conferred the status of truth, thereby elevating the speaking subject to that of Historical agent. Victims are not, for instance, cross-examined. Their stories are duly recorded, as spoken, in the official archive. In the interests of reconciliation and in exchange for representational agency, however, the witnessing victims are expected to forego or convert any demands for retribution.

Indeed this form of settlement has its proximate basis in the Universal Declaration of Human Rights. It is not coincidental that the first freedom to appear in the Preamble to the Universal Declaration is that of speech. This first freedom, as Joseph Slaughter argues, is not simply one among a litany of others, but rather it serves as the anchor for all the rights that follow: "the liberty to tell one's story is precisely what the thirty articles of the Universal Declaration attempt to ensure through prohibitions of abuses that tend to destroy the human voice — negative rights — and through promotions of social welfare that tend both to encourage and to foster the human voice speaking itself — positive rights."[7] If the liberty to tell one's story is the foundation of the UDHR, it is noteworthy that immediately following the appearance of this first freedom, the next preambular paragraph situates this promotion of the voice as a preemptive measure against the possibility that "other actions" might be undertaken as a response to tyranny and oppression. The third preambular paragraph reads as follows: "*Whereas* it is essential, if a man is not to be compelled to have recourse, as a last resort, to rebellion against tyranny and oppression, that human rights should be protected by the rule of law."[8] Acts of rebellion thus serve as the explicit negative in the advancement of the codified principles of human rights. Such acts are the limits against which the telling of one's story — representing oneself — serves as the mechanism of substitution. Within these institutional constraints the narratives of political terror delivered before the commission are expected to produce a cathartic effect that will convert the violence described in order to generate a (legal) therapeutic resolution. In this way, we might say that *testimonio* supplants testifying in the courts of reconciliatory justice.[9]

As this brief synopsis suggests, the Truth Commission form has a close relationship to the literary. Indeed a host of scholars have considered precisely such structural consistencies. In her book *Barred: Women, Writing and Political Detention,* for example, Barbara Harlow argues that the thirty articles of the UDHR "translate[] the standard literary paradigm of individual versus society[,] . . . recharting the trajectory and peripeties of the classic *bildungsroman.*"[10] And as Allen Feldman has argued of the South African Truth and Reconciliation Commission, "in many ways the [TRC] was intended as the *status confessionis* writ large to compass the entire nation as a collective witness and mass confessing agent."[11] Conversely, as this transit between narrative forms and the human rights inquiry suggests, the field of the literary (or perhaps thinking the literary) is also affected by the dilemmas confronted, negotiated and generated by the Truth Commission. As Barbara Harlow and David Atwell have recently written:

> South African literature since 1990 has taken upon itself the task of articulating this larger predicament [of the "transition"]. Its fields are the experiential, ethical, and political ambiguities of transition: the tension between memory and amnesia. It emphasizes the imperative of breaking silences necessitated by long years of struggle, the refashioning of identities caught between stasis and change, and the role of culture — or representation — in limiting or enabling new forms of understanding.[12]

This larger predicament of the transition relates directly to the warning that Allen Feldman has issued about this type of institutional memory theater and its historicity: "To enclave the human rights violation story at a primordial scene of violence is already to preselect the restorative powers of legal, medical, media, and textual rationalities as post-violent."[13] And in the context of the "new" South Africa, poet and former political prisoner Jeremy Cronin rearticulates and transposes this problematic onto a broader geopolitical grid:

> The three political contexts of the South African conflict, as elaborated in the Report (apartheid, the Cold War, and the African anti-colonial struggle) are also all conveniently in the past. Apartheid has, constitutionally, been removed; the Soviet bloc has collapsed; and the formal European colonization of Africa is no longer a reality (with arguable exceptions like the French occupation of Mayotte). Once again the implicit message is that the struggle is over. The internal and external impediments that isolated us from the world and that blocked the emergence of a unified, new South Africa/South Africans have now disappeared. But have they?[14]

With this rhetorical question Cronin signals the presence of a specter of nonconvertibility that haunts the official, historical periodization into past and present. In the process he figures the concept of "the transition" as a *catechresis* deployed to project a future in which "the struggle is over."[15]

Being suspicious of presumptive declarations of a new day and keeping the struggle alive is what animates the critical project to question the representational borders erected between past and present. As a critical rejoinder to the official politics of the Transition, I set out here to show how this representational aporia is made manifest in the incontrovertible force of violence that inevitably wins out in the form of critical tensions of nonconvertibility. Such critical thresholds continue to haunt the political economy of conversion in the spectral form of a finality without end: "there is no liberation from violence" and "there is no such thing as nonviolence."[16] Such anti-ideal conclusions do not augur the death of politics nor preclude "having a desire or tendency to escape violence, to reduce its forms and lower its levels," but it does trouble and render ambivalent our relation to any absolute ethical principles of overcoming or universal solutions.[17] As we have seen, Balibar argues that extreme violence arises not only against institutions but also from within them. "Absolute" choices, e.g.," between a violent or a nonviolent politics, or between force and law," do not allow escape from this circle. He therefore concludes that the only "way" out of the circle is "to invent a politics of violence, or to introduce the issue of violence... into the concept and practice of politics."[18]

Insofar as the Truth Commission remains within the delimited horizons of political reason carved out in the Universal Declaration, the invention of such a "politics of violence" out of such an institution is a dead letter. And there is ample reason to suppose that such will be the case for some time to come, given the hegemonic installation of the absolute principle of nonviolence into human rights practice since the Mandela affair (see chapter 1). And yet, the repeated encounter of the Truth Commission with the strict limits of (non-)convertibility has compelled a critical reckoning that, even advocates admit, renders the Truth Commission a less desirable option of redress and in need of critical rethinking.[19] That is to say, insofar as the Truth Commission theater reinstalls the traumatized subject at the center of the historical process, the fact that "this installation will not disinstall violence from history" means that the pursuit of alternatives will necessarily continue. To the extent that the form of the Truth Commission as determined by the ideology of human rights remains more or less locked in a judicial frame of limited value as a mode of critique on the state's monopoly on violence and its dominant representations, we must look elsewhere for the ways in which demands for justice overflow the limits of official history and its memory theaters.[20]

At the same time, even erstwhile critics like Feldman suggest that there are no guarantees that Truth Commissions will necessarily or wholly advance the interests of the state. Instead he suggests that Truth Commissions may also unleash forces that are not easily contained within the official protocols:

> ... to the same degree that such disseminated narrative products may be viewed skeptically as having a distorted relationship to historical knowledge, we have to acknowledge that neither human rights inquiries and commissions ... absolutely dictate the condition of narrative production from political emergency zones where multiple forms of political agency have emerged and survive. The legal formalization, media virtualization, and commodification of witnessing constitute cultural-economic formations, rehabilitation agendas and patterns of denial and forgetfulness that can foreclose our recuperation of historical depth and complexity. At the same time they also navigate and unavoidably open for potential critical inquiry an ambiguous and often horrific historical terrain that is not easily contained by legal rationality, curative resolutions, and consumer desires.[21]

What form might such openings take? What kind of historical terrain do they "unavoidably open for potential critical inquiry"? Toward a consideration of these questions, in the remainder of this chapter I consider two literary texts that have produced, albeit in very different ways, important signs of the nonconvertibility of violence into nonviolence. The first is a play written by Ariel Dorfman in the aftermath of dictatorship in Chile entitled *Death and the Maiden* in which the persistent tension between (private) justice and (national) reconciliation is played out under the sign of hysteria. A second text of somewhat ambiguous generic form, a chronicle of tyrannicide written by Claribel Alegría and Darwin Flakoll entitled *Death of Somoza* details the actions of a group of Argentinian commandos as they successfully carry out a plot to kill the deposed Nicaraguan dictator Anastasio Somoza Debayle. As texts that produce signs of nonconvertibility, each can be read as informing the narrative politics at work in the project of building and maintaining a counterpublic archive. What such a representational politics might mean for the dispossessed is difficult to interpret, but in their insistence to look outside the juridical instance, from below and beyond the nation-state, they help to expose the fragile foundations of a geopolitics of humanity and its new theatrical structures, which include the institution of the Truth Commission.

The Hysterical Present

When the coding of organized public violence breaks down and the conversion of violence is disturbed, the state enters a period of extreme crisis — as is the case when Law and Terror become synonymous and resistance is liberated from its dominant coding as just so many forms of criminality. When as a result of such of breakdowns, the political form of state is overthrown or must change, through bloody or bloodless revolt, by coup or electoral plebiscite, the field of violence is subject to reorganization. Unless the means of violence is distributed throughout the social field (as Luxemburg argued it should be), the task of the official discourse of Transition is to rehabilitate the code of public violence and reinstall the field of legitimate and illegitimate uses of violence *in the interest of the state*.

To challenge this unwanted ending for a justice yet to come, the task of critical, "antijuridical literatures" is to animate the specter of nonconvertibility and refuse the conversion of state violence into nonviolence and its transfer into political institutions. In her exemplary account of the politics of "the Transition" in Chile, cultural theorist Nelly Richard says of this conjuncture:

> The consensual model of a "democracy of agreements" formulated by the Chilean government of the Transition (1989) marked a passage from politics as antagonism (the dramatization of conflict governed by a mechanism of confrontation under dictatorship) to a politics of transaction (the formula of a pact and its techniques of negotiation). The "democracy of agreements" made consensus its normative guarantee, its operational key, its deideologizing ideology, its institutionalized rite, and its discursive trophy.[22]

One of the earliest and most internationally acclaimed literary texts to emerge out of the tensions of transition in Chile, following the end of the Pinochet dictatorship, came from the well-known author and cultural critic Ariel Dorfman.[23]

Dorfman's award-winning play *Death and the Maiden* had its world premiere at the Royal Court in London in 1991.[24] Originally written in Spanish, *La muerte y la doncella* opened in Santiago later that same year.[25] The play comprised three acts, divided into eight scenes, and performed by three characters. In an afterword to the play included in the English-language publication and dated September 11, 1991, Dorfman recounts that he began the play "eight or nine years" earlier "when General Augusto Pinochet was still dictator of Chile" and Dorfman himself was still in exile.[26] At that time he had in mind a dramatic situation involving a woman who reencounters a man who had raped and tortured her in the aftermath of the 1973 coup d'état. What he says "he could not figure out" at the time, however, was "who the woman's husband was, how he would react to her violence." The scenario lay dormant for nearly a decade. It was not until "Chile returned to democracy in 1990" and Dorfman himself returned to his home country that he finally figured out how the story "had to be told." What was lacking in those interim years? What became possible (and necessary) in the context of a transition? Why was a "third perspective" necessary at all and what kind of ideological work did its inclusion in the drama make possible? Just how did this third perspective afford a way out of the dramatic impasse?

Upon the return of democratic rule, Dorfman decided that the husband would be a member of the Rettig Commission, established by the first postdictatorship president, Patricio Alywin, to investigate the crimes of the dictatorship. The play's characters were thus determined: Paulina Salas, a woman around forty years of age and victim of torture, Roberto Miranda, a doctor and presumed torturer, and Gerardo Escobar, Salas's husband and a lawyer appointed to the human rights commission. With this trio in mind, Dorfman set out to examine, what he called, the difficult "transition to democracy" where "so many Chileans were grappling with the hidden traumas of what had been done to them while other Chileans wondered if their crimes would now be revealed."[27] However, as Dorfman knew, the task of establishing the truth of what happened that fell to the commission was always already deeply compromised by the specific conditions of the transition in Chile wherein Pinochet was "still in command of the armed forces, still able to threaten another coup if people became unruly or, more specifically, if attempts were made to punish the human rights violations of the outgoing regime."[28] And, most importantly for him, "in order to avoid chaos and constant confrontation, the new government had to find a way of not alienating Pinochet supporters who continued occupying significant areas of power in the judiciary, the senate, the town councils — and particularly the economy."[29] The stability of the postdictatorial government thus rested on carefully negotiating the class and ideological divides that lorded over the transition as officials sought to instantiate a new lease on the monopoly over the field of violence and its historic rebirth.

The mandate of the commission reflected the uneasy terms of this historic transition, as its investigations were limited to only those crimes of the dictatorship that "ended in death or its presumption," and it would "neither name the perpetrators nor judge them" (72). In some of his more recent nonfiction writings, Dorfman praised this compromise (calling it a "prudent but valiant course between those who wanted past terror totally buried and those who wanted it totally revealed"), all the while recognizing that "justice would not be done and the traumatic experience of hundreds of thousands of other victims, those who had survived, would not be addressed" (72). His play, in turn, would go beyond the practical limits of good governance into aesthetic realms where the possibility of a more extensive catharsis and healing might be staged. Here he would pose the sort of questions that the new democracy could not, but which simmered just below the surface of the cautious public discourse:

How can those who tortured and those who were tortured coexist in the same land? How to heal a country that has been traumatized by repression if the fear to speak out is still omnipresent everywhere? How do we keep the past alive without becoming its prisoner? How do we forget it without risking its repetition in the future? Is it legitimate to sacrifice the truth to insure peace? And what are the consequences of suppressing the past and the truth it is whispering or howling to us? Are people free to search for justice and equality if the threat of a military intervention haunts them? And given these circumstances, can violence be avoided? And perhaps the greatest dilemma of them all: how to confront these issues without destroying the national consensus, which creates democratic stability? (73–74)

Ultimately, it is the specter of nonconvertibility that Dorfman's *Death in the Maiden* places before the altar of this drama of reconciliation.

Prior to the introduction of the third term of nonviolence the only dramatic solution was that the torturer should be punished if not killed and the tortured should be the one to perform the deed. In other words, without the figure of nonviolence, there would be no means of converting the logic of violence, which inexorably led to retribution, within which the victim–perpetrator dyad was enclosed. Beginning, as Dorfman did, from the premise that violence is not an option, or at least not a desirable one (insofar as he conceives it as antithetical to "democratic stability"), the insertion of a third term is absolutely necessary. Paradoxically, however, Dorfman's sympathies (tortured as they may be) appear to reside with Paulina's desire for retribution; the third perspective is figured in the character of Gerardo, who is, at best, pathetic and, at worst, a lying, hypocritical, egomaniacal idiot. What was it then about the way that Dorfman imagined the field of possibilities that required him to side, in the last instance, with the clownish figure of Gerardo? For this, we need to consider how we reached such an impasse in the first place.

Death and the Maiden opens under the specter of hysteria with the torture victim, Paulina Salas, reaching for a gun as car lights approach her beach vacation home. Shortly after this opening figure of paranoid fear, Paulina and her husband, Gerardo Escobar, discuss the utility and the limits of a newly established truth and reconciliation commission. Gerardo has been appointed by the recently elected president to serve on the commission created to facilitate the passage from "dictatorship to democracy." Paulina suspects a betrayal. In the opening salvo of this exogamous exchange, Paulina cross-examines her commissioner-husband on the prescribed and delimited form of the Chilean Truth Commission:

> PAULINA: This Commission you're named to. Doesn't it only investigate cases that ended in death?
> GERARDO: It's appointed to investigate human rights violations that ended in death or the presumption of death, yes.
> PAULINA: Only the most serious cases?
> GERARDO: The idea is that if we can throw light on the worst crimes, other abuses will also come to light.
> PAULINA: Only the most serious?
> GERARDO: Let's say the cases that are beyond—let's say, repair.
> PAULINA: Beyond repair. Irreparable, huh?
> GERARDO: I don't like to talk about this, Paulina.
> PAULINA: I don't like to talk about it either.[30]

The mounting tension evident in this repartee marks the beginnings of an inexorably widening gap between the official techniques of conversion and that of Paulina's experience of victimization. And yet, at this early juncture, and for a brief and fleeting moment, both voices are poised to countenance the possibility of a dialogical bridge in the name of truth and its promise:

> PAULINA: Find out what happened. Find out everything. Promise me that you'll find everything that ... —
> GERARDO: Everything. Everything we can. We'll go as far as we ... (*Pause.*) As we're ...
> PAULINA: Allowed.
> GERARDO: Limited, let's say we're limited. But there is so much we can do.... We'll publish our conclusions. There will be an official report. What happened will be established objectively, so no one will ever be able to deny it, so that our country will never again live through the excesses that ... (10).

While the prospect of recording the truth of what happened animates Gerardo's faith in preventing future excesses, Paulina senses a bypass of more pressing desires, an impending bureaucratic death brought to bear upon the past in the name of a future that looks remarkably similar. The apparent gap will come to be seen as an aporia over which practical and official reason will have no purchase. It is the relative certainty of continuity between past and present that induces Paulina's "increasing hysteria":

PAULINA: And then?
Gerardo is silent.
You hear the relatives of the victims, you denounce the crimes, what
    happens to the criminals?
GERARDO: That depends on the judges. The courts receive a copy of
    the evidence and the judges proceed from there to —
PAULINA: The judges? The same judges who never intervened to save
    one life in seventeen years of dictatorship? Who never accepted
    a single habeas corpus ever? Judge Peralta who told that poor
    woman who had come to ask for her missing husband that the
    man had probably grown tired of her and run off with some other
    woman? That judge? What did you call him? A judge? A judge?
*As she speaks, Paulina begins to laugh softly but with increasing
    hysteria.* (10)

Paulina's demands for justice *will be* betrayed by the commission.
From this moment forward, the private voice for justice and the
official institution of Transition drift further and further apart. The
limits of the commission and the betrayal that such limits entail take
on profound significance when Paulina comes to suspect that her
torturer, Doctor Roberto Miranda, has, quite by accident, appeared
in her home. Suddenly the possibility of another form of doing justice becomes available. It is through the figure of female hysteria
thus unmoored from the practical limits of national reconciliation
that this other scene of domestic politics is staged.

In an interesting but problematic analysis of the Polanski/Dorfman
film version of *Death and the Maiden* (1994), literary theorist Idelber
Avelar takes the writer/director to task for hystericizing the female
despite the "obvious gesture toward feminism" involved in the way
such hysterics play off against the idiocy of the (male) voice of reason. As Avelar correctly says, Gerardo comes off as "almost mentally
retarded."[31] Even though Paulina's hysteria is shown to be warranted
and Gerardo's reasonableness a mask for sheer self-aggrandizing,
Avelar insists that the script/film pushes the pseudo-feminist character too far into madness to ever receive a hearing for her suspicions.[32]
And while we do need to critique the privatization/interiorization
gendering of the figure of hysteria, it is also (and successfully) the
sign for a sense, both paranoid and reasonable (that is to say, indeterminate), that there is no justice to come in the designs of the future as
mediated through the Truth Commission. In this way, hysteria functions as a sign of the persistent specter of nonconvertibility in which

the past is grasped as still very much alive. Hysteria, then, serves as the incontrovertible negative force to the insistence of official conversion that seeks to break the present from the past in the name of a new future. Against the dictates of official conversion, it marks the uncertain outcome of the future and keeps alive the question of the past-ness of the past that renders the present (and future) as a site of contestation and struggle. It is through the figure of hysteria, and its immanent reasonableness, that the right to recall the past in the future is maintained and is not (and cannot be) handed over to the demands of transition, reconciliation, and consensus.

Indeed once Paulina is satisfied that there is no good reason, or reasonable good, standing between her and the possibility of justice outside the Law, she is restlessly drawn toward a final solution:

> PAULINA [*interior monologue*]: And why does it always have to be people like me who have to sacrifice, why are we always the ones who have to make concessions when something has to be conceded, why always me who has to bite her tongue, why? Well, not this time. This time I am going to think about myself, about what I need. If I only do justice in one case, just one. What do we lose? What do we lose by killing one of them? What do we lose? What do we lose?[33]

At this moment, and despite all the dramaturgical signs pointing to an ending that will leave, as the title intimates, only death and the maiden, Paulina is nevertheless denied the possibility of converting the cruelties of the past through retributive violence. Indeed by the point of this interior monologue, Paulina seems to have resolved any lingering doubts or concerns, and the only thing left to determine is the mode of killing. And yet it is at this point that Dorfman freezes the scene — the point at which his fantasies for another ending threaten to dissolve the possibility of future reconciliation — adumbrating the aporia between the two voices for justice with the cacophonous sounds of dissonance:

> *They freeze in their positions as the lights begin to go down slowly. We begin to hear music from the last movement of Mozart's Dissonant Quartet. Paulina and Roberto are covered from view by a giant mirror which descends, forcing the members of the audience to look at themselves. For a few minutes, the Mozart quartet is heard, while the spectators watch themselves in the mirror. Selected slowly moving spots flicker over the audience, picking out two or three at a time, up and down rows.* (66)

This is a tragic moment in the play, not strictly speaking because of what happens (in some sense it might be said to avoid tragedy), but because it is a false ending, disingenuous to a fault, a capitulation to an exteriority that enters to veto everything that has preceded it and impose a condition of stasis on characters and audiences alike. Where I do have a problem with this figuration is not in its hystericization, but in its sacrificial conversion into nonviolence and its silenced transfer into the institutions of bourgeois culture. Dorfman, mistakenly, gives to this exteriority an air of a necessity:

> And yet, even as my imagination ran rampant, even as I savored a society turned upside down and inside out, where the hunted of yesterday became the hunters of today, even in a play where the author supposedly can write whatever he wants, I found myself reluctantly prodding Paulina toward an ending she did not want and I did not want and yet was there, waiting for her and the people of Chile: My protagonist, having tried to bring some personal measure of justice to the world, sits down, when all is said and done, in a concert hall in close and uncanny proximity to the doctor she thinks damaged her irreparably, both of them sharing the same space, the same music, the same peaceful and miserable and lying land. In *Death and the Maiden,* I could not, Paulina could not, fantasize another ending.[34]

His abrupt foreclosure on this other scene of politics appears as a moment of dissatisfaction, the "unwanted ending," the ending to which all (characters, author, and audience), in piecemeal fashion (the light "picking out two or three at a time") are forced to submit. Unable to convert the specter of retribution into either legitimate or preventative counterviolence or maintain its force as an incontrovertible historical memory, Dorfman hands us over to what cultural critic Nelly Richard has aptly described as "the center function" which designates "the generic name of a new configuration of political space, a free unfolding of consensual power that corresponds to the free apolitical development of production and circulation."[35]

What Dorfman misidentifies as a practical necessity runs counter to the possibility of either critical distance (as a more Brechtian ending might allow) or collective solidarity (as the Boalian theater of the oppressed might prefer). The dropping of the mirror between characters and audience shatters the possibility of both. Within the refractions of the Enlightenment speculum, we are left only with a false universality and the fiction of (national) community. His unwillingness to "fantasize another ending" is the result of an inability to conceive of a politics of violence outside the framework of a Restoration. Under such terms, the possibility of a preventative counterviolence *for the future* is rendered inconceivable and forcibly negated — installing unfreedom at the heart of the aesthetic, as Adorno might say. What is thus restored is the Law itself, which the discourse of transition, for all its gestures toward a new beginning and a new future, is designed to preserve. Our identification, in the last instance, is with the state. And the principled commitment of human rights to nonviolence reinforces this identification even as it, and we, "struggle against excessive violence in all its forms."[36] So while Dorfman has, on the one hand, produced a figure that should, by all accounts, defy the demands of official conversion, he has, on the other hand, sacrificed this figure in, and to, the juridical process. And it is here that the charge of pseudo-feminism may have its strongest application, not in the figure of hysteria itself, but in the negation of what the hysteric knows: the contradictions involved in forgiving the unforgivable. Such a negation recasts the force of nonconvertibility as an episode scheduled for eventual overcoming with all the political anamnesis that such a historiographic gesture entails.

And Pinochet? Despite more than a decade long pursuit by human rights lawyers and victims of his brutal dictatorship, he never stood trial for his many crimes against humanity. And on December 10, 2006, at the age of ninety-one, he died in a Santiago hospital surrounded by his loving family.

Exiting the Structures of the Juridical

The forced resignation of Anastasio Somoza Debayle on July 17, 1979, marked the end of nearly fifty years of dictatorial rule over Nicaragua by the Somoza family, which formally began when the elder Somoza, Anastasio Somoza García, deposed Juan B. Sacasa, his uncle by marriage, from the presidency in 1934.[37] A year earlier, at the urging of the United States (which occupied the country from 1912 to 1933), the newly elected President Sacasa appointed Somoza García director of the Guardia Nacional (a constabulary force organized by the U.S. marines). In 1934 Somoza moved to consolidate his control on power when, during peace talks with the popular leader of the rebellion against the U.S. occupation, Augusto César Sandino, he had Sandino assassinated. Less than two years later, Somoza García forced Sacasa from office and installed himself as dictator. For the next twenty years (1936–56), until his assassination by the journalist and poet Rigoberto López Pérez, Somoza ruled Nicaragua with an iron fist, all the while amassing an enormous family fortune through slaughter, theft, and official decree. This family tradition, with its stalwart support from the north, continued right up until the third member of the dictatorial dynasty, Somoza Debayle, boarded the early morning plane on July 18, 1979, for Homestead Air Force Base in Miami.

In the waning months of the Somoza dynasty, the depths of the tyrannical tradition were on full display. Following an unsuccessful insurrection by the Sandinista National Liberation Front (FSLN) in September 1978, Somoza ordered the indiscriminate air bombardment of six major cities in a vain and vicious attempt to keep the Sandinista guerrillas from consolidating power. The air campaign left more than 50,000 dead (80 percent of them civilians), 100,000 wounded, an estimated 40,000 orphaned, and some 150,000 refugees who fled north to Honduras and south to Costa Rica. In the final days, when his downfall appeared inevitable, Somoza and his closest associates "systematically siphoned off all the loose cash in the country, leaving the Central Bank with reserves of only ... 3 million dollars."[38] It was a sum "sufficient to keep the country running for two days" (3). Despite Somoza's own claims that he "followed the plan of the United States word for word" as to how to orchestrate the transfer of power (in order to keep the Sandinistas out of power), his successor departed from the script, much to the chagrin of Washington, and Somoza's welcome was withdrawn.[39] His search for an exilic home ultimately landed him in Paraguay, a country still firmly under the dictatorial control of General Alfredo Stroessner.[40] From outside the halls of sanctioned American power, another plot was in the works that would alter the course of Somoza's retirement. It is this other plot that Claribel Alegría and Darwin Flakoll set out to reassemble for the counterarchive.

In contrast to the traumatic tropology and unwanted ending of Dorfman's *Death and the Maiden,* Claribel Alegría and Darwin Flakoll's non-award-winning *Death of Somoza* (1993) chronicles the actions of a small group of commandos as they carried out a successful mission to execute the deposed Nicaraguan dictator, Anastasio Somoza Debayle. Based on interviews with the seven Argentinian survivors who performed the deed, the Salvadorean-born Alegría and her partner and translator Flakoll dramatically reconstruct the events leading up to and immediately following the 1980 assassination. Similar to *Death and the Maiden,* the text of *Death of Somoza* opens at the point where the human rights report leaves off, but in this text the "human rights option" does not return in the end to prescribe the limits of practical action or reason. Before the story begins, the authors' preface is preceded by the "Conclusions" from the OAS "report on the Situation of Human Rights in Nicaragua" (1978). Under the heading of "Time Capsule" the veritable end of the human rights report serves as the point of departure for the political thriller. The "Time Capsule" image is important insofar as the metaphor designates the kind of official representation for the future that the human rights document performs, in contrast to the narrative which follows that will serve as a historical counterarchive for the unofficial future.

While the conclusion of the official document encapsulates the "serious, persistent, and generalized violations" carried out upon Nicaraguan society under Somoza ("especially those persons of limited economic resources and young people between the ages of 14 and 21"), it ends with little more than a gesture toward a future evolution to human rights equity: "the damage and suffering caused by these violations have awakened in a very forceful way, an intense and general feeling among Nicaraguan people for the establishment of a system which will guarantee the observance of human rights." The limits of the official human rights report are figured in a structure of feeling that will, it is hoped, provide a bulwark against any "future" return of extreme state violence. Here, the dissatisfactory ending is placed at the beginning as that which is to be gone beyond in the interests of a different articulation of justice. No truth commission was formed in Nicaragua as the revolutionary government of the Sandinistas took over power, and no sanctioned international tribunal was involved in the legal pursuit of Somoza.

While the question of ethical violence provides the better part of the dramatic tension in Dorfman's fictional psychothriller ("should she torture him? should she rape him? should she kill him?" etc.), the outcome of this narrative is announced from the outset: *Somoza will be assassinated.* Chapter 1 reiterates the truth of the title as it begins with Somoza's exilic flight to Miami and ends with the foreboding fact that "he had exactly fourteen months to live."[41] We have full knowledge of what will happen, so much of the dramatic tension within the narrative is provided through the narration of who these people were, how they came to imagine this as a possibility, and, most centrally, how they implemented it as a reality. But in addition to the narrative tension, a larger dramatic tension persists behind the very selection of this subject as a story that deserves to be told. On the one hand, this is a very old story; chronicles of tyranni-cide date back at least to the time of the murder of Hipparchus by Harmodius and Aristogiton in ancient Athens, which became the popular representational subject of various *scolia* (drinking songs) and commemorative works of art from statues to histories for cen-turies. Indeed, any defense of tyrannicide could well count on the support of such great names of intellectual antiquity as Pliny, Theog-nis, Herodotus, Xenophon, Plato, Aristotle, Demosthenes, Plutarch, Lucian, and Cicero, to name but a few advocates. The long and dis-tinguished classical and medieval traditions of intellectual advocacy run well into the modern age through Milton and on up to, at least, Thomas Jefferson — who once famously announced that "the tree of liberty is nourished with the blood of tyrants."[42] On the other hand, since the age of democratic revolutions, and especially since the middle half of the twentieth century when the concept of crimes against humanity emerges, open intellectual support for tyrannicide has diminished dramatically. So while the deed may enjoy consider-able popular appeal, its symbolic representation must navigate the tension produced through the opposition between law and terror and the presence of new theaters of punishment beginning with the Nuremburg Trial. As Alegría and Flakoll announce at the outset, "This story is not an apology for terrorism, but rather the chronicle of a tyrannicide."[43]

As the chronicle from the other side opens, it is not histori-cal emplotment that positions the structure of the narrative, but geography. Three of the Argentinian protagonists are in a small fishing village near Barcelona awaiting a call from the Sandinistas in response to the commandos' offer to come to Nicaragua to sup-port the struggle to overthrow Somoza. A fourth person is in a hotel in Panama, also awaiting word, while three others, in exile and dispersed throughout Europe, begin to prepare for a journey to Nicaragua. It is May 1979. Add to this mix a couple of writers from El Salvador, and the makings of a countergeopolitical mapping of transnational solidarities becomes possible and necessary. In a short time, the entire group converges on Managua, "united again, the years of European exile ended" (20). It is "Ramón" (the pseudonym given to the leader of this group of ERP members, Enrique Haroldo

Gorriarán Merlo) who first articulates the historic significance of this regional sense of solidarity:

> We have always kept in mind that Latin America, during the epoch of Spanish colonization as well as in the present phase of imperialism, has had the same enemy. The heroes of the first independence, among them San Martín and Bolívar, had a Latin Americanist attitude. San Martín's soldiers shed their blood in Chile and Peru, and Bolívar's in Colombia, Ecuador, and Venezuela. That is to say that the heroes of the first independence saw the Latin American revolution as one single thing. For them, each Latin American country that liberated itself from Spanish colonialism signified an advance in the revolutionary process that was developing in their own countries.... We are partisans of this concept.... For us, there is no difference between fighting for the liberation of Nicaragua, El Salvador or Argentina. (25–26)

As the possibility of a counterrevolution loomed on the horizon with Somoza announcing his plans to return to Nicaragua from Paraguay within six months, three of the commandoes hit upon an idea of how they might be able to support the revolution:

> "...It would be a historic disgrace to permit the murderer to die peacefully in bed."
>
> "Armando is right," Santiago chimed in. "Somebody ought to wipe him off the face of the earth."
>
> "Very well, *compañeros*..." Ramón paused to give more weight to what he was about to say. "In that case, why don't we have a go at it?" (29)

As Alegría and Flakoll recount how the idea for tyrannicide came about, ethical considerations intrude as a momentary interruption in the plot design. Quite tellingly, that is, the protagonists appear relatively unburdened by the moral quandaries of violence as an absolute ethical limit. "Ramón" interjects the weighty question in the form of an afterthought:

> "But we're getting ahead of ourselves. First of all, do either of you have any objections to taking this job? Any moral qualms, let's say?"
>
> Santiago shook his head definitively.
>
> "We'd be doing a favor to humanity," Armando erupted. "We've seen the horrors Somoza committed here: the mass graves, the young men in the street with both hands chopped off, the thousands of innocents he killed with indiscriminate bombardments. For my part, I think that all these tinhorn dictatorships should be taught that revolutionary justice never sleeps and they can no longer get away with their

crimes and then leave the country to settle down peacefully with their stolen riches and their bodyguards."

"We'd be doing a great favor to the Nicaraguan revolution," Santiago mused.

"And not only that," Ramón added, "but it would be a crushing demonstration of Latin Americanist solidarity that would send chills down the backs of the Pinochets, Videlas and the rotating dictators here in Central America." (32)

No moral deliberations will, from this point forward, impinge directly upon the narrative account of this antijudicial guerrilla act. Neither the discourse of human rights nor that of the law in any explicit form will reappear as frameworks of containment (literary or otherwise) in this text. This attempt to displace law, and its trance-like ideological effects, as the starting point marks an attempt to liberate the chronicle from any preemptive ethico–juridical short-circuits.

The questions and meaning of solidarity, like the meaning and significance of the planned deed, are subject to multiple articulations given the collective nature of the testimonio. When "Susana" first finds out that she is going to be part of a mission to kill Somoza, she readily admits that the idea caught her by surprise. She had fully anticipated that the training she was undergoing was directed toward an operation back in Argentina, not Nicaragua. "I'll admit that the idea of the operation stunned me," she says. "At the beginning it seemed simply incredible. I began to realize that everything we preached for years, international solidarity, was also involved here." But perhaps more important than her expression of surprise was her conception of the deed: "It was a way," she said, "of carrying out a definitive act of justice, just as Rigoberto López Pérez had done with Somoza's father" (44). Describing tyrannicide as "a definitive act of justice," suggests that the significance of the act, including its moral significance, begins and ends *with the action*. In other words, in this formulation, there is no other end toward which the action is directed. It is not instrumental in that way. It does not have that kind of rationality behind and after it. It is not figured as part of a preventive counterrevolutionary measure. It is a sheer manifestation of justice.

Such a noninstrumentalized act of justice serves as an opening onto a counterconception of solidarity that refuses the opposition between speech and rebellion as figured in the UDHR. "Ana" expresses it this way:

> I was taught...that revolutions are not only national, but also con-
> tinental and international movements. Che taught us that with the
> concrete example of his entire life.... He taught us that when demo-
> cratic forms of expression do not exist, armed struggle is the only
> valid response to dictatorship.... all through the continent [revolu-
> tionaries] are perfectly clear that when people are denied free political
> expression, armed struggle is the only valid answer. (44–45)

Alegría and Flakoll's re-presentation of a multiplicity of voices
involved in the same deed helps to sustain the heterogeneous meanings that the act can have, both for those involved and those distant.
This helps prevent any sort of simple conversion of the act into an
absolute framework where its meanings might be reduced to this or
that singularity.

In fact, instead of trying to contain the representation of violence
as an ethical threshold, Alegría and Flakoll must attempt to mini-
mize the violence of representation as narrative limit. That is to say,
it is in the act of representation, of re-presenting the deed, as *theatrical event,* that it becomes subject to an economy of conversion that
threatens to undermine the very sense of imaginative possibility that
the text attempts to keep alive. In other words, the ideological opening effected by the deed, the sense of possibility it breaches, becomes
subject to a foreclosure in the act of narration, insofar as the format
(spy-type thriller) threatens to perform a conversion of the ordinary
subjects into extraordinary actors (the exceptional hero). As a way
to write against such an untoward ending, Alegría and Flakoll give
the last words to the ordinariness of the commandos:

> I think it's very important that you say this: that you show that we
> who executed Somoza are not highly-trained super agents. We are
> *compañeros* who experience fear and whose fearlessness does not lie
> in thrill-seeking nor in taking risks. We are revolutionaries with all
> the fears, the doubts, the failings, the problems, that everyone else
> has. We quarrel amongst ourselves, and in the moment of action, our
> legs tremble. Not in the moment of action, but ten minutes later, our
> legs tremble. (151–52)

We should read this figure of fear and trembling and its placement
at the end of the story (as epilogue), as seeking to prevent the tex-
tualization of the event — with all its overtones as a spy thriller —
from heroicizing the protagonists in ways that would distinguish,
differentiate, and otherwise distance them from the people in whose
interests they acted. The danger to be warded off is that the act of

narration will contribute necessarily to the epic aggrandizement of
the protagonists and their conversion into exceptional individuals.
Against this danger, the authors put forth supplemental preventative
articulations near the close of the chronicle:

> ... not a single one of us ever wanted to be identified. The only way
> Ramón's identity became known was because of a violation of con-
> fidence on the part of a newspaperman. This is a measure of the fact
> that nobody wanted to boast about our participation in the oper-
> ation. The more anonymous we remained, the better, not only for
> reasons of personal security but because none of us had any interest
> in achieving notoriety. (149–50)

Again the placement of these testimonio elements at the end of the
text is critical to a representational strategy in which the unwanted
epic-effect of the chronicle (and the spy thriller narrative format) is
continually worked over and against. There are no hysterics here;
there are no markers of distinction that would work to separate the
commandos except that which inheres in the narrative act. There
are only passions, fears, concerns, loves, commitment, barbecues,
and intensities; all of which serve to help avoid the transposition of
the deed, as crime, onto another plane, where criminality is used to
break any unities between the dispossessed and their heroes.[44]

In the end, the publication of Alegría and Flakoll's account would
have to wait more than a decade. Despite having completed the
manuscript by 1983, the authors were asked to shelve the text until
the conditions for reception were right. Specifically, Ramón, the
leader of the commando group, asked them to postpone the publication of the book because the collapse of the Argentine dictatorship
had created a new situation in that country wherein the People's
Revolutionary Army (ERP) had "opted for a line of peaceful political action."[45] Under this strategic directive it was believed that the
publication of the book "might foment polemics and recriminations
best laid aside in a country that was seeking to restore an image of
civility" ("Preface"). The authors heeded the request and put the
text on the shelf. This is a particularly important request insofar
as it underscores the *strategic flexibility* behind the commandos'
approach to what is to be done in any specific context. That is to
say, such strategic flexibility signals that they have no particular or
necessary "preference" for violence, and given a certain conjunctural configuration of force, they are more than willing to pursue a

path of negotiation and dialogue, all the while reserving the right, in the last instance, to use violence if the situation dictates.

Against official demands for a break with the past, the act of tyrannicide is here figured as a means of working upon the past. As an act of historical justice, it works upon the past, not as a means of determining the future, but as a means of doing justice for the dead. As Ana says in the epilogue: "the worst thing that could have happened to Somoza had already happened, and that was to have been dethroned. It seemed to me important that he should pay for the terrible crimes he had committed. We felt that the project was inspiring, a way of doing justice for all the violent deaths and all the injustices that are committed each day in Latin America" (149). Or again, as "Armando" suggests, "we have to resolve a historical problem" (151). Ultimately the act of tyrannicide and its representation in this text work against a means–ends framework that would instrumentalize the action and deny the very possibility of counter-violence and the production of a counterarchive. As a chronicle that attempts to displace the ethical question as a substitute for the political, the counterarchive works to keep alive the imagining of possibilities beyond what is sanctioned, beyond what it is possible to say out loud and publicly, beyond the juridical instance. The historiographic injunction at work in the chronicle is one of keeping the past alive, working in and upon the past, as a politics of the present and for the future. The struggle was alive, is alive, and will be alive. To determine whether the act has any instrumental value as a political strategy is beside the point. Or rather it misses the point. It is, we might say, more accurately understood as a sheer manifestation of solidarity.

It would be another five years before Alegría and Flakoll said that they began to think of publishing the chronicle once more. Again, however, political events intervened and strategies abruptly changed course. Early in 1989 Ramón and his group of Argentine leftists carried out an attack on La Tablada fortress in Buenos Aires, killing a score of Argentine military personnel. The time of publication was again postponed. To be clear, I recount this here to signal something of the unique status of this text insofar as the conditions that informed and mediated the publication of the account were driven by a political calculus, and not, as would likely be the case if it were simply a journalistic rendering, a market calculus. As an act of solidarity, the authors subordinated publication concerns to a consideration of the impact that the text might have on ongoing conflicts in the Americas. Finally, in 1993 the tactical time was right, and the chronicle of the tyrannicide was published.

It is perhaps more, rather than less, important in our contemporary context to distinguish forms of state and revolutionary violence and to work in those troubling areas where determinations are less than clear. I don't want to suggest that Alegría and Flakoll's negation of bourgeois justice is without complications or that Dorfman's unwanted ending should commit us to a simple preference of one over the other. Instead, both texts stage in important and interesting ways the challenges that come from outside the law, as well as the residues of popular justice that cannot easily be converted into civil and political institutions. In their ex-centric relation to institutional politics, both texts evidence and reject any simple, absolute decisions such as choosing between a violent or a nonviolent politics or between force and law. Just as Feldman has suggested that we read the human rights testimony as "testimonials to the irreconcilable," it is both possible and necessary to read these two texts in a similar vein.[46]

While the question of the (non-)convertibility of violence into political institutions has long animated revolutionary traditions of thought and practice from Marx to Lenin, Luxemburg to Fanon, Mao to the Zapatistas, and beyond, it has made a hasty retreat in the halls of metropolitan theory under the formidable weight of the hegemony of the idea of nonviolence. And while the historical persistence of state and insurgent violence across the twentieth century — through the experiences of revolution and counterrevolution, fascism and antifascism, decolonization and neocolonization, and the emergence of the neoliberal empire and its opponents — necessitates a critical engagement with this dynamic tradition of debate, it is a *postconflictual* ethos that has come to rule over the question of violence and its (non-)convertibility. In an epistemological coup of no small import, the *logos* of democracy has been ushered in, despite the realities of its historical record, as the very antithesis to state violence and the formal project to which everyone, except the most recalcitrant and backward-thinking, must submit. The rule of theoretical law appears to demand nothing less, and if we return against the grain to pose the question of the non-convertibility of violence in relation to democracy, it is not out of any obstinate desire to cling to the revolutionary past or to cast the anarchistic deed as the privileged revolutionary stratagem, but rather to recognize that *the barbaric* has flourished in the hallowed institutions of the democratic as much as in the minds and totalitarian regimes of madmen and tyrants from Stalin to Bush. We all, in various ways, desire an end to violence, but the problem of violence is not undone by giving ourselves over to the ironclad Law of the nonviolent (if even it were possible) and indeed such a relinquishing may do more to contribute to the persistence of tyranny than to its elimination.

5

Combat Theory
Anti-imperialist Analytics since Fanon

Proof for the United Nations

In a pivotal scene from Gillo Pontecorvo's 1966 anticolonial epic *The Battle of Algiers*, Ali La Pointe, petty criminal-cum-revolutionary, ascends the stairs of one of the many safe houses of the Algerian quarter with Ben M'Hidi, a leader of the ALN forces (the armed wing of the FLN) in Algiers. It is the eve of a seven-day general strike organized by the Algerian National Liberation Front.

LA POINTE: We can't do anything for a week.

M'HIDI: What do you think of the Strike?

LA POINTE: I think it'll succeed.

M'HIDI: I think so, too. It's been well organized. What will the French do?

LA POINTE: Obviously, they'll try everything to break it.

M'HIDI: They'll do more than that, because we've given them an opportunity. You know what I mean? Now they'll no longer be groping in the dark. Every striker will be a recognizable enemy, a certified criminal. The French will take the offensive. Understand what I mean?

LA POINTE: Yes.

M'HIDI: Jaffar says you weren't in favor of the strike.

LA POINTE: No, I wasn't.

M'HIDI: Why not?

LA POINTE: Because we were ordered not to use arms.

M'HIDI: Acts of violence don't win wars; neither wars nor revolutions. Terrorism is useful as a start. But then, the people themselves must act. That's the rationale behind this strike, to mobilize all Algerians, to assess our strength.

LA POINTE: To prove it to the UN?

94

M'HIDI: Yes, to prove it to the UN. It may not do any good, but at
least the UN will be able to gauge our strength.

The contradictions in the FLN strategy of trying to access the structures of international recognition and enter the universal realm
of humanity in the midst of a revolutionary war proved to be
catastrophic in the film as it had in reality.

In the year leading up to the call for a general strike in January 1957, the FLN had intensified its urban guerrilla war against
the French occupation of Algeria in an attempt to bring the long-
standing resistance in the countryside to the capital city with its
one million *pieds-noirs*. In January alone, the ALN executed more
than one hundred attacks in the capital itself (although the primary fight remained in rural areas with more than four thousand
attacks around the country during the same month). The success
of the hit-and-run operations, coupled with the recent expansion of
the United Nations General Assembly with seventeen states mostly
from the Eastern bloc or Afro-Asia gaining membership in 1955,
and the Cold War maneuverings of the United States, catapulted
"the Algerian Question" onto the international stage. In an attempt
to leverage the UN debate, the leadership of the FLN decided that
they needed to demonstrate the falsity of the French claim that
the militants "represented nobody" and were simply "a bunch of
terrorists."[1] As Pontecorvo's film narrates the battle, however, the
decision to try to carry the struggle to an international arena carries
grave consequences for both the organization and many thousands
of its civilian supporters. As M'Hidi fears in his exchange with Ali la
Pointe, the French seize upon this opportunity to crush the militant
cadres. Upon hearing the news of the strike, "Colonel Mathieu,"
the French commander in *The Battle of Algiers,* says: "Now we can
lick them. They have made their first bad move."

In the twelve-day period encompassing the strike and its immediate aftermath, some seventy-seven thousand people were tortured in
the city of Algiers, as the counterinsurgency identified and destroyed
cell after cell. The distinguished theorist and consultant to the film
Eqbal Ahmad argues that the idea of the general strike, which
since the late 1800s and the early 1900s had been a very effective proletarian tactic in Russia and throughout parts of Europe
(as Luxemburg theorized), was misguidedly superimposed on the
situation of revolutionary warfare in Algeria. Revolutionary warfare, Ahmad contends, differs from conventional warfare insofar

as the mass of the population must "officially remain neutral" and cannot be seen as taking sides. In order to protect people, "revolutionaries must maintain the fiction of popular neutrality"; "good revolutionary tactics always create an environment in which the people are overtly neutral, while covertly larger and larger numbers of them support the revolution by various means."[2] While successfully demonstrating the breadth of popular support for independence and the capacity of the FLN to organize the people on a mass scale, the general strike exposed nearly the entire Algerian population to attack. Following this critical strategic error, the FLN was systematically annihilated, and the French went on to victory in the Battle of Algiers. Adding insult to torture, the UN advanced a vacuous resolution on the Algerian question calling for "a peaceful, democratic, and just solution . . . conforming to the principles of the United Nations charter." A declaration hardly worth the enormous sacrifices made back in Algiers.

Combat Theory

The contradictory relation between anticolonial violence and international recognition received its most elaborate postwar theorization in the last work of Frantz Fanon, *The Wretched of the Earth*.[3] In this text, Fanon advanced a very distinctive conception of violence and one that has been frequently misunderstood, in no small part owing to the monumental scope of the political project set forth. In this classic treatise for the decolonizing world, the revolutionary intellectual from Martinique categorically rejected the terms of Western values and the parameters of Western epistemology. "The European game is finally over," he defiantly declared. "We must look for something else."[4] The call to stop looking to Europe for models of progress or the means to salvation was not, of course, Fanon's alone, but rather was a part of a mass postwar movement of the third world against the West. This systematic postwar resistance to the Empire *as West,* as Edward Said aptly characterized it, was marked by a recognition that no Western-generated value, no esteemed ideal, no system of thought, and no political practice had escaped the contradictions of centuries of imperialism and its colonial spiritual adventure.[5]

In Fanon's account, he argues that no movement inside Europe had been able to successfully build a different kind of humanity across the international divisions of the colonial world, despite having produced "all the elements for a solution to the major problems of humanity."[6] The most likely ally in this internationalist project, the European proletariat, had repeatedly missed the opportunity to break with European adventurism and forge a new kind of dialogue or a new kind of relationship with their superexploited, non-European counterparts.[7] The call for the proletarians of the world to unite had proved inadequate to interpellate the European worker over and against the material crumbs and ideological grandeurs of progress, as "European workers ... believed [that] they too were part of the prodigious adventure of the European spirit" (237). Thus it was time, according to Fanon, for the third world to discard the false notions of progress, development, and humanity, which Europe offered up as the means to liberation and set out on an entirely new path not yet made, but very much in the making.

In order to understand the anticolonial analytic that Fanon advanced in *Wretched of the Earth,* we need to grasp the unique theorization that he gave to the concept-word "violence." In particular Fanon argued that the nature of violence in the colonies was such that it carried with it a politico-intellectual obligation to *take sides*. The committed nature of his theoretical insurgency has prompted a range of postwar intellectuals to either downplay or ignore Fanon's analytic of violence or to attempt to disentangle it from its partisan charge. As a recent example of this latter type of move, Samira Kawash argues that Fanon "actually makes it impossible to choose, for violence or against, because there is no singular determination of violence in Fanon's text."[8] In her terms, the "impossibility to choose" issues from the way that the violence of decolonization as figured in *Wretched of the Earth* is "always in excess and elsewhere to the instrumental violence of the colonized in struggle" (237). Kawash casts this violent doppelganger as a "spectral excess ... not reducible to ... particular violent acts," a purely immaterial violence. (238)

This is a sophisticated intellectual move in which Kawash tries to tease out two distinct senses of violence in Fanon's *Wretched,* which are otherwise collapsed under the singular heading of "violence." While such a distinction affords the postcolonial intellectual an anxiety-relieving loophole large enough to drive a phantom truck through, there are two major problems with this theoretical maneuver: first, it guts Fanon's work of its critical, disruptive force; and second, there is no evidence, textual or otherwise, that supports the contention that Fanon draws a distinction between material and immaterial violence. In fact, the violence of decolonization, like that of imperialism, materializes all the time; *what remains immaterial is our ability to read it.* Rather than collapsing the question of decolonizing violence into undecidability by making recourse to the spectral, Fanon's materialist hermeneutic *obliges* the revolutionary intellectual to align with the very real praxis of the colonized in violent struggle, in the making of a new politico-epistemological project.

This intellectual obligation derives from recognition of the totality of colonial violence and the social differentiations it produces. The given culture of the colonized world is wholly and inextricably constituted in and through colonial violence: an ontological condition in which every social relation — economic, cultural, physical, and imaginary — is organized by violence. Indeed in Fanon's analysis, violence is the form of relationality itself, from the micrological to the macrological and the molecular to the molar. There is no outside, no exteriority, no space that exists free from the life and death worlds that colonial violence has created and reproduced over time. In other words, borrowing from the later theorization of power put forth by Michel Foucault, we might say that relations of violence for Fanon "are not in a position of exteriority with respect to other types of relationships (economic processes, knowledge relationships, sexual relations) but are immanent in the latter; they are the immediate effects of the divisions, inequalities, and the disequilibriums that occur on the latter, and conversely they are the internal conditions of these differentiations."[9] In contrast to Foucault, and in the interest of reconfiguring Hegel's dialectic and Marx's hierarchy of determinations, however, Fanon argues that in the colonies relations of force are thoroughly racialized such that "the economic substructure is also the superstructure, the cause is the consequence; you are rich because you are white, you are white because you are rich."[10] The stretching here of Marx is not, as it would be later for Foucault, toward a microphysics that is without predication or structure, but toward a conception of a given culture in which the micro- and macro-logical organization of life and death stems "from the racial denial of any common bond between the conqueror and the native."[11] A denial, as the postcolonial theorist Achille Mbembe argues, that "in the eyes of the conqueror" constitutes "savage life [as] just another form of animal life...something alien beyond imagination or comprehension."[12] Race not only regulates the boundary between the human and inhuman in Fanon's conception, but is constitutive of an originary colonial violence that in its founding institutes a sphere of law and right out of which "humanity" emerges as the negation of savage life. The inhuman conditions of a given colonial culture, as well as the inhumanity of the colonized, are established via a violent, racialized ordering in which the totality of colonial violence secures a relation between knowledge and power that necessitates a politico-intellectual practice of differential engagement (not identification) involving a critical dismantling of the intellectual's own formation in relation to both the state and the popular. In this, there is no question of "choosing" nonviolence over violence.

In order to confront this totalizing form of colonial instrumentality, Fanon argued for the use of the very same *technē* that defines the form and field of relationality in the colonies: violence. Despite concerns from various quarters (then and now) that such a strategic injunction only escalates the cycle of violence, Fanon was decidedly unconcerned with any possible appearance of symmetry between colonial and anticolonial violence. For him, colonial violence simply had no equivalent. Instead, the *apparent* paradox of using violence to confront violence served as a systemic provocation to the long durée of European Enlightenment thought, which insists upon the need to promote various notions of transcendence as the means to freedom (from Kant's categorical imperative to the Frankfurt School's critical reason and beyond). Indeed Fanon uses the very same concept-word "violence" to designate both the colonial form of domination and the anticolonial form of resistance, precisely because he refused to advance the latter as a transcendent form of praxis.

The Gift of Recognition

Decolonizing violence in Fanon's formulation must be affirmed because the limits and failures of nonviolent recognition have been demonstrable within the global, colonial capital machine from the slave plantation to the colony to the occupied territory. Such a critical understanding was first articulated at the close of *Black Skin, White Masks* with his account of the life and death politics of recognition in the master–slave dialectic under the heading of "the Negro and Hegel." What Fanon argued at this early juncture was the necessity of *forcing* recognition from the Other and not simply making appeals for it or having recognition conferred by the Master. The costs and consequences of a nonviolent confrontation are not, as is frequently supposed in contemporary Fanonian scholarship of the psychoanalytic variety, primarily borne by the colonized subject *qua* subject in the aborted form of a nontherapeutic resolution. Rather, failure to force recognition means that the slave — of whatever historic form — will remain in roughly the same position after emancipation. Fanon allegorizes the historic tragicomedy as follows:

> One day a good white master who had influence said to his friends, "Let's be nice to the niggers...."
>
> The other masters argued, for after all it was not an easy thing, but then they decided to promote the machine-animal-men to the supreme rank of men.
>
> Slavery shall no longer exist on French soil.
>
> The upheaval reached the Negroes from without. The black man was acted upon. Values that had not been created by his actions, values that had not been born of the systolic tide of his blood, danced in a hued whirl around him. The upheaval did not make a difference in the Negro. He went from one way of life to another, but not from one life to another.... The white man, in the capacity of master, said to the Negro, "from now on you are free."[13]

As long as the power to confer or withhold the recognition of the Other's humanity remains a decision made elsewhere, there will be no substantial alteration of the material conditions that serve as the basis for the very possibility of a distinction between the human and the inhuman.[14] What Fanon suggests here is that all appellative modes of recognition and/or redress are doomed to reproduce the power of the state and the cultural–economic structures indispensable to the smooth functioning of racist–colonial capitalism.[15] As Fanon's closing allegory in *Black Skin, White Masks* figures the problem of nonviolence, it is in the absence of actional struggle to the death that the Negro is handed over to constitutional freedom under the Law, and there he or she remains subject to the exploitative vagaries of the gift.

Despite the allegorical register (master–slave, settler–native, etc.), which Fanon frequently deploys to dramatize the politics of recognition, it is necessary to situate the "new" subjectivity that decolonization makes possible in relation to the entire field of force that constitutes the inhuman conditions of global, colonial capitalism.

By the time of *Wretched of the Earth*, Fanon argues that the "thing" becoming man, the native now animated by the violence of decolonization, requires a direct confrontation with the material and symbolic force field organized by the colonizer into distinct spaces of development (the famous figure of the "Manichean world" most starkly realized in settler colonies, but not entirely absent from the general order of historic and contemporary capitalist societies). Thus in *Wretched*, Fanon's opening series of declarations about the absolute necessity of decolonizing violence is immediately followed by a description of the sociospatial economy (the "inhuman conditions") of the colonial world:

> The colonist's sector is a sector built to last, all stone and steel. It's a sector of lights and paved roads, where the trash cans constantly overflow with strange and wonderful garbage, undreamed-of leftovers. The colonist's feet can never be glimpsed...they are protected by solid shoes in a sector where the streets are clean and smooth, without a pothole, without a stone. The colonist's sector is a sated, sluggish sector, it's belly is permanently full of good things. The colonist's sector is a white folks' sector, a sector of foreigners.[16]

This is the starting point, the immediate "context," without which one cannot begin to understand how the glorified "humanity" of the colonizer and the despised "inhumanity" of the native have been materially and symbolically reproduced at every turn and in every facet of living and dying in the colonies. The inhuman conditions of settler–colonial capitalism are made evident in the contrasting figures of the overabundance and hyperdevelopment of the European sector and the deprivation and underdevelopment of the native sector and its death-world: "you are born anywhere, anyhow. You die anywhere, from anything." You live in a "world with no space, people piled one on top of the other, the shacks squeezed tightly together." It is a famished sector that "crouches and cowers...a sector of niggers [and] towelheads" (4). In this cramped sector "riddled with taboos," the colonized can only gaze upon the colonist's sector with envy, replete with untoward dreams of possession. Even the unconscious domains of the imagination and of physicality do not escape the world that colonial violence has made, as they too are constituted by the systematic ordering of the management, reproduction, and control of social reality in the colonial world. As Mbembe has more recently written of colonial territorialization:

> Colonial occupation itself was a matter of seizing, delimiting, and asserting control over a physical geographical area — of writing on the ground a new set of social and spatial relations. The writing of new spatial relations (territorialization) was, ultimately, tantamount to the production of boundaries and hierarchies, zones and enclaves; the subversion of existing property arrangements; the classification of people according to different categories; resource extraction; and, finally, the manufacturing of a large reservoir of cultural imaginaries. These imaginaries gave meaning to the enactment of differential rights to differing categories of people for different purposes within the same space; in brief the exercise of sovereignty. Space was therefore the raw material of sovereignty and the violence it carried with it. Sovereignty meant occupation, and occupation meant relegating the colonized into a third zone between subjecthood and objecthood.[17]

The violent processes of colonial territorialization remake the ground upon which the entire colonial edifice is built, establishing a chain of power that can be broken only once "the great organism of violence . . . has surged upward in reaction to the settler's violence."[18]

The totalitarian character of colonial exploitation is not, according to Fanon, content with the physical delimitation of the colonized; instead the native is figured as "the quintessence of evil," "the enemy of all values," whose "mere existence 'deforms' all values" and "disfigure[s] all that has to do with beauty or morality."[19] In fact, in Fanon's account, the native is so completely constituted by the absolute excess of colonial violence (physical, symbolic, epistemic, etc.) that it matters little whether any particular action by the colonized (from dreams of possession to suicide bombing) might be read or perceived as violent (and therefore illegitimate), because the native always already appears *as violence*.[20]

Palimpsestic Time

Since the publication of *Wretched* and his youthful death a few months later, Fanon's work has circulated about the world, serving as a critical tool for those engaged in decolonizing struggles and influencing a wide range of intellectual theories and movements. In recent decades, however, the critical reception of Fanon in the West has been largely adumbrated by a more dominant tendency in which the question of the nation has been eclipsed by the "forces" of "globalization, transnationalism, even postnationalism."[21] These metropolitan theoretical developments have advanced quite rapidly since the end of the Cold War despite the formidable expansion of U.S.-led imperialism (corporate–financial and military) and the aggressive recolonization of neocolonial states. The retreat from the nation-state and revolutionary critique is part and parcel of a more general theoretical drift toward a "new cosmopolitanism" distinguished, as Pheng Cheah argues, by "the attempt to ground the normative critique of nationalism in analyses of contemporary globalization and its effects."[22] Against this cosmopolitan tendency, however, M. Jacqui Alexander has recently outlined a very useful way of rethinking the "transnational," wherein the contemporary global field is treated as a composite formation comprised of a series of shifting relations between three different kinds of state formations: the colonial, the neocolonial, and the neoimperial.[23]

In her critical reckoning with what she calls the "palimpsestic time"[24] of these modern state forms, Alexander argues that *no* state formation (no matter how democratic, socialist, or communist, in form or practice) falls outside the determinate structures of modernity's violence nor are any "positioned to circumvent the nexus of violence — neither the violence through which they are constituted nor the regulatory disciplining practices that they animate" (194). In this formulation any and all attempts to lay claim to the status of the exceptional are systematically refused, in favor of foregrounding the "connective web [of coercion and violence] within and among colonial, neocolonial, and neo-imperial social formations" (194). As she outlines this critical project, contra cosmopolitan transnationalism, we have to attend to the simultaneity of, and linkages between, contemporary state forms:

> Since both neocolonial and neo-imperial states work, albeit asymmetrically, through colonial time and simultaneously through Christian neoliberal financial time — organized under the auspices of global capital interests and lending agencies such as the International Monetary Fund and the World Bank — our task is to move practices of neocolonialism within the ambit of modernity, and to move those of colonialism into neo-imperialism, reckoning, in other words, with palimpsestic time.

In contrast to the developmentalist models of state forms and the conceptions of linear time that subtend the various iterations of contemporary cosmopolitanism, Alexander's concept of palimpsestic time works against the (implicit) hierarchies of modern state formations. It is, however, not surprising that those nations and regions that have long proclaimed their superiority over the rest of the world would continue to be the sites from which theoretical models are (re)produced that position certain nation-states and state forms as the most advanced while relegating other forms to a state of perpetual backwardness or, in a more paternalistic vein, to a condition of catching up (or as some like to say, "developing").[25]

In the midst of this latest postwar cosmopolitan advance, with the revolutionary politics and alternative temporalities of decolonization more or less banished from debate, the sole superpower, the United States, launched the Gulf War in January 1991. Despite the slaughter of more than 220,000 Iraqis in the first six weeks of the war and the "almost apocalyptic devastation [of] Iraq," many leading Western intellectuals "ranging from Habermas to Lyotard, and from Dahrendorf to Bobbio...maintained that the war was...justified."[26] A large majority of Western public opinion also accepted the war as necessary and desirable, likely owing in part to the legitimation of the war by the UN Security Council. This unprecedented international sanctioning of multilateral mass slaughter in the early years of the post–Cold War era was soon followed by "the first humanitarian war" near the close of the decade when the largely unrivaled leader of the West and its NATO associates carried out the 1999 bombing of Kosovo.[27] Taken together these two military operations, with their complex rearticulation of the relations between imperialist violence, international law, and the global human, mark a significant concatenation of powers at work toward a long future of cosmopolitan wars to come. In other words, the U.S. bid for monopolistic control over the capacity for terror (real terror, not the spectral kind), which began in earnest with the 1945 bombings of Hiroshima and Nagasaki, has at least for the near future been more or less realized. The superimposition of U.S. military power over the entire global field of force has given this particular nation-state extensive capacity to lead and direct the "connective web of coercion and violence" across and between colonial, neocolonial, and neoimperial structures of domination.

Despite the fact that violence of countless heterogeneous forms (subjective, objective, structural, systemic, and symbolic) constitutes an all-pervasive feature of our globalizing, "postnational world," its theorization in a revolutionary modality has fallen into utter disrepute. This theoretical paradox has by and large failed to grab the attention of Western intellectuals, save for a scant few who have recognized, as does Étienne Balibar, that "there is certainly a good case to be made that the looming counterrevolutionary or counterinsurrectional character of massive violence calls for a 'counter-counterinsurrection,' a renewal of the idea of revolution." And yet, even Balibar hesitates: "There is a difficulty here: that of falling back into the very *symmetry* of political methods and goals that, since the first socialist and anti-imperialist revolutions attempted to seize power in the name of 'the dictatorship of the proletariat,' has helped extreme violence become built into the very heart of emancipatory politics and helped the twentieth century become...the 'Age of Extremes.'" As a result of this wariness, he suggests that "it is not only the *state* or the *economy* that needs to be 'civilized' or to become 'civil' but also *revolution itself.*"[28] In our "postsocialist age" this constitutes one of the more sympathetic critiques of "revolution" that otherwise underpins the selectivity and wariness with which the revolutionary theorists of decolonization — Césaire, Fanon, Cabral, Rodney, etc. — are received or ignored today.

Beyond the debates within the history of Fanon studies, then, critical engagement with Fanon's work suffers from its placement within a more generalized crisis in which it is supposed that the violent projects of decolonization, like the projects of state socialism and postcolonial national independence to which they bear a certain uneasy affinity, have largely failed, and thus it is time to look to social movements and civil society for more contemporary (and less contaminated) forms and practices of emancipatory politics.[29] But for the practice of human rights, this emancipatory potential has itself been thoroughly imbricated in the "new military humanism," insofar as the latter draws substantial ideological cover and sustenance from the rhetoric of human rights. Having been largely woven into the fabric of neoimperialism, the option of purification, so rigorously pursued in the early years of nongovernmental human rights, appears off the table. And indeed it is this crisis of entanglement that is driving the search for an alternate paradigm for human rights.[30] For my part, then, it is not out of nostalgia that I return here to engage the materiality of violence in Fanon's work, but rather to reconsider how his politico-epistemological project attempts to articulate a different kind of international urgency and solidarity, from below and to the left, whose central praxis of liberation is not located in the transcendent struggle for autonomy (in the form of individual or political sovereignty) but in the immanent struggle against "the generalized instrumentalization of human

existence and the material destruction of human bodies and popula-
tions."[31] Understood in this way, nothing seems to me *less* outdated
than the work of Fanon and the by-now classic decolonizing ideal
of justice he advanced.

Against Cosmopolitanism

In his insistence on thinking the totality and necessity of violence,
Fanon's anticolonial analytic quite usefully cuts against the grain of
the hegemony of the nonviolent and offers us an important foundation from which to engage an emerging body of critical work
devoted to examining how colonial cleavages and asymmetries have
been rearticulated "after colonialism" through various postwar,
international institutions and discourses. Such a critical project distinguishes a number of important recent theorizations, including
those of Danilo Zolo on the United Nations and International Tri-
bunals, Pheng Cheah and Balakrishnan Rajagopal on international
human rights, M. Jacqui Alexander on international solidarity, and
China Miéville on International Law and international legal theory.[32] This emergent, post–Cold War body of works constitutes a
collective critical movement directed toward understanding the time
and forms of the present through the long history of modernity's
violence. In each analysis, the question of the postwar international
is engaged from the histories of imperial/colonial violence that have
given particular shape and form to the expressed ideals of peace,
order, and justice — idealizations that persistently obscure the law-
making and law-preserving function of international institutions
thereby leaving the violence of such functions hidden beneath the
humanist sign of the cosmopolitan. While postwar Western humanism tended to assume that some form of universal human rights
was necessary to overcome the international divisions of humanity
(colonial, ethnic, cultural), Fanon's postwar engagement with the
West challenged the idealized figure of "Man" and "the human" on
the grounds of its very *constitution* through colonial violence. The
work of Alexander, Cheah, Miéville, Zolo, and others continues in
this vein in a counteranalytical genealogy to contemporary studies
in the fields of international relations, international law, and political science that assume that some form of supranational institution
based on the UN Charter model is indispensable for the realization
of the ideals of global and human justice.[33] In a direct challenge to

this assumption, the Italian political philosopher Danilo Zolo suggests a different point of critical departure: "Can any cosmopolitan project ever be anything other than an inherently hegemonic and violent undertaking?"[34]

In his critique of actually existing cosmopolitan models, Zolo argues that the United Nations was the third in a series of world-historic attempts to secure peace and stability on a global scale, preceded by the Holy Alliance (1815) and the League of Nations (1920). What he demonstrates is that over the past two centuries each successive attempt by powerful nations to devise an international scheme to ensure lasting and universal peace, however "genuine" in its ambitions, has consistently run up against a primary interest in the maintenance and expansion of the hegemonic power of those states whose victory in a continental or world war had just been won. The result? "None of the three schemes," Zolo says, "has achieved any notable degree of success." Indeed the effects have been quite the opposite, as both real world conflict and the potential for conflict have expanded immensely. The contradiction between the (stated) "desire for peace" and the (actual) "quest for hegemonic power," it seems, overdetermines the logic of international institution-building. What becomes clear in attending to this history of failure is that "in constructing new forms of concentration and legitimation of international power, [victorious powers] have time and again attempted to hold in check those movements which — arising principally from technological and economic developments — militate against the continuation and legitimation of their own control."[35] Rather than creating conditions for peace or advancing the development of a new humanity, each "new" cosmopolitan model worked to extend the power of the recently victorious nations: Austria, Great Britain, Prussia, and Russia after the Napoleonic Wars; Great Britain, France, Italy, and Japan after the First World War; and the United States, Great Britain, and the Soviet Union at the close of the Second World War.

In the latest reconstruction after the Cold War, it is the United States that has largely directed attempts to rearticulate "the international" through the paradigm of a "New World Order." The consequences of this rearticulation, from the first Gulf War to the invasions of Afghanistan and Iraq, have been all-too-predictable, as "the entire structure of the existing international institutions" has come to serve as a critical instrument in "the diplomatic preparation for, and formal legalization and legitimation of, war" (43). Once again the imperial–cosmopolitan attempt to overcome the "statist" fragmentation of international power through a military–political structure and a highly centralized jurisdiction serves as the very means to expand the international aggression of the powerful and intensify the force of their destructive effects.

Zolo thus concludes that, in practice, the attempts to establish a "universal and lasting peace" tend "to go hand-in-hand with a freezing of the world's political, economic and military map as it is at the time of the constitution of the organization."[36] This, he maintains, is "because the idea of peace is opposed not only to war but also, implicitly to the notion of social change, development and productive rivalry." While Zolo may overstate the degree to which such international restructurings actually "freeze" the "world's political, economic, and military map," he is correct in suggesting that the pressure from hegemonic powers exerts a great deal of force toward maintaining and expanding existing lines of power and control. Nevertheless, the differential management of force is subject to counterhegemonic pressures that give to the "international division of humanity" a dialectical dynamism largely erased in Zolo's metaphoric freezing.[37] Does this dialectic suggest that International law might be an arena for progressive intervention?

This is the subject of the award-winning horror/science fiction/fantasy writer China Miéville's wide-ranging account of international law and international legal theory, *Between Equal Rights: A Marxist Theory of International Law* (2005). Miéville's nonfictional theoretical debut is organized around the question of whether international law has any progressive or radical emancipatory potential. As he notes, very few legal theorists, even those most critical of international law, are willing to abandon this arena as one worthy of struggle. Rather, there is a deep investment in trying to mine international law for some space of possibility, some space of maneuver, out of or through which a progressive politics might be advanced. The notable critical legal theorist B. S. Chimni, for example, argues that "the realm of law [is] not the arena from which struggle for radical changes could be launched," but that nevertheless "the legal system provides diverse tools to deal with the perils which face mankind." Or again, legal scholar Martti Koskenniemi claims that while there "is no coherent project for a better world" in International law, international lawyers "should be normative in the small" as they take part in a more general emancipatory project. In what Miéville refers to as the most intriguing of recent theorizations from within international legal scholarship, Peter Fitzpatrick argues that while the law's "determinate content" will respond to "the demands of predominant power," such law can still "pose a ruptural challenge to "imperium" by virtue of its constituent ethics."[38]

In each critical theorization from within international legal scholarship the quest is to identify that space within, or opened up by, international law that is appropriable by progressive or radical forces. And despite differences in the various critical accounts, this space is presumed to emanate from the law's insistence on equality, freedom, and impartiality. In other words, given that the international legal form assumes the juridical equality of its subjects, namely sovereign states, the politico-strategic question thus becomes what is the relation between this juridical equality and the unequal violence of sovereign states? Against this directive to wrest juridical equality from coercive force, Miéville argues that when and where the form of juridical equality appears, in effect, to triumph over the unequal violence of imperialism, imperial powers simply ignore the (nonbinding) decisions, maintaining as they do, monopolistic control over the terms of application. They got us coming and going, as the familiar saying has it.

Thus while select critical legal theorists have begun to readily acknowledge and take up the imperialist foundations of international law, they tend to retain a steadfast belief in the need for supranational institutions of law. The ideological form of legal cosmopolitanism thus establishes a certain critical limit beyond which critique is believed to descend into anarchy or nihilism.[39] These politico–epistemic thresholds, the absolute limits of modern liberalism, establish the terms of the unthinkable and the unethical. For Miéville on the other hand, these absolute limits are precisely what need to be rethought, and so he advances, á la Fanon on decolonization, a series of absolute declarations: international law "cannot and will not act to further a 'just world order' "; international law is structurally incapable of acting as a transformative force for justice; "without imperialism there could be no international law"; etc. Like Fanon, Miéville advances an understanding of the totality of imperialism, and it is this conception of totality that leads him to refuse any aspect of the imperial enterprise, including the derivations of international law, as being subject to reform, amendment, or progressive appropriation. No aspect of international law, in Miéville's formulation can be supported, even if apparently beneficial or superficially progressive: "To try to pick up the pieces of imperialism to support and others to condemn is to fail to deal with it as a totality." Any emancipatory appearance of this or that decision is never the result of a calculus in which equality or humanity has triumphed over power and imperialism; rather the universalizing logic of international law is inextricably bound up in the maintenance and extension of imperial violence over international relations, and this is consistent throughout the history of international law.

Increasingly, it is to human rights discourse that scholars and activists turn in their attempts to identify where international law might be most subject to appropriation by the progressive left. In general alignment with the concerns about human rights raised in this book, Miéville argues that "even if one agrees that such a discourse might provide space for a radical critique of power, that is not *all* it does."[40] In his terms, the susceptibility of human rights to "counter-appropriation, even when able to wrest a progressive effect, far outweighs any radical appropriative possibilities." As he writes:

> The point is not that the substance of particular conceptions of human rights cannot be marshaled to progressive discourse. The point is that the attempt to appropriate the international law of human rights for that project is precisely abstracting of that substance and thus abstracted is easily reappropriated by those in power. In addition, because "the human rights regime...is composed of more than those legal rules and institutions that explicitly concern human rights," such an "appropriative" approach by implication legitimates not only specific other laws which may even facilitate or excuse human rights abuses, but the very edifice of international law and juridical forms that has been so swingeingly [*sic*] criticized (sometimes by those now attempting to appropriate the categories).[41]

While Miéville acknowledges that it would be "fatuous to deny that law could ever be put to reformist use," such "progress" (as Marx once argued) is always "hedged by retrogression." The meager chance of provisional, progressive appropriation via human rights, coupled with the certainty of grave costs in the form of legitimizing the very structure of international law and in promoting a false understanding of what international law is and does, prompts Miéville to counsel in favor of forms of struggle from below that leave the realm of international law and work "against the rule of law."[42]

Coda

The Transition from Dumb
to Smart Power

At the January 2009 U.S. Senate confirmation hearing, Secretary of State Hillary Clinton laid out her ideas for how to advance U.S. interests in the post-Bush era. At the center of her proposal was what she called "smart power": "We must see what has been called smart power, the full range of tools at our disposal — diplomatic, economic, military, political, legal, and cultural — picking the right tool or combination of tools, for each situation."[1] According to Clinton, smart power recognizes that "international law and international institutions are tools that help us to promote and advance our interests and values, not traps that limit American power," and that "the Bush administration ha[d] presented the American people with a series of false choices: force versus diplomacy, unilateralism versus multilateralism, and hard power versus soft." "Seeing these choices as mutually exclusive alternatives," she argued "reflect[ed] an ideologically blinkered vision of the world that denies America the tools and the flexibility necessary to lead and succeed."[2] After eight years under George Bush, such an "enlightened" agenda must have had the ring of a decidedly new direction in foreign policy.

The author of the phrase "smart power," Suzanne Nossel, was apparently pleased with Clinton's use of the concept: "Hillary was impressive. She didn't gloss over the difficulties, but at the same time she was fundamentally optimistic. She's saying that by using all the tools of power in concert, the trajectory of American decline can be reversed. She'll make smart power cool."[3] At the time Nossel coined the term "smart power," she was vice president of U.S. Business Development at the international media conglomerate Bertelsmann, having previously served as deputy to the ambassador for UN management and reform at the U.S. mission to the United Nations

(1999–2001).[4] Nossel is currently chief operating officer of Human Rights Watch.

In her original formulation, Nossel advanced the concept of smart power as a means to "revive liberal internationalism," which she said had to be "reinvented" after the neoconservative Bush regime had "entangled the rhetoric of human rights and democracy in a strategy of aggressive unilateralism."[5] As a result of this "taint[ing] of liberal internationalist ideals," she argued, "progressives . . . must reframe U.S. foreign policy according to their abiding belief that an ambitious agenda to advance freedom, trade, and human rights is the best long-term guarantee of the United States' security against terrorism and other threats" (135). For neocons who might have been concerned that the United States was actually changing course, Nossel offered reassurance: "building a broad-based liberal internationalist movement will not force the US to give up the driver's seat" (137).

For his part, President Obama has also been quite assertive about the need for an imperial restoration following the dark ages of the Bush years, as he declared during his campaign:

> The secret authorization of brutal interrogations is an outrageous betrayal of our core values, and a grave danger to our security. We must do whatever it takes to track down and capture or kill terrorists, but torture is not a part of the answer — it is a fundamental part of the problem with [the Bush] administration's approach. . . . Torture is how you set back America's standing in the world, not how you strengthen it. It's time to tell the world that America rejects torture without exception or equivocation. . . . When I am President we won't work in secret to avoid honoring our laws and Constitution, we will be straight with the American people and true to our values.[6]

Subsequently charged with the mandate of "reversing America's decline" both at home and abroad, the Obama administration quickly moved to soften the edges of U.S. imperialism. On his very first day in office, President Obama signed an executive order to close the torture chamber at Guantánamo Bay, making good on his promise to ban the illegal and immoral use of torture. This move, widely supported even by top-ranking military officials, took aim at the (unnecessary) "excesses" of the previous regime with the substantial ideological windfall of normalizing and routinizing the more fundamental operations of imperial occupation in Iraq and Afghanistan. But just in case this largely symbolic action might appear weak in the face of the terrorist threat, Obama made clear that this did not signal any sort of retreat in the "war on terror" but merely constituted part of a more strategic reorganization predicated upon the superlegalization of the imperial mission: "the message that we are sending around the world is that the United States intends to *prosecute* the ongoing struggle against violence and terrorism [my emphasis]." And again, if there were any lingering concerns about a more fundamental change in U.S. foreign policy, such anxieties were quickly laid to rest when, on day four, the new president unilaterally authorized two missile strikes in Pakistan killing an estimated twenty-two people.[7]

The use of missile strikes is apparently not the only "counter-terrorism tool" to survive the transition from Bush to Obama, as the new president also moved within his first two weeks in office to issue an executive order granting the CIA authority to continue the practice of "rendition" (the secret snatching of suspects off the street, anywhere in the world, without any due process, and the "rendering" of them to secret holding locations in other countries).[8] The Obama administration has evidently determined that the rendition program, despite considerable opposition from around the world, is necessary in the "war on terror."[9] As one anonymous Obama official put it:

> Obviously you need to preserve some tools — you still have to go after the bad guys. The legal advisors working on this looked at rendition. It is controversial in some circles and kicked up a big storm in Europe. But if done within certain parameters, it is an acceptable practice.[10]

In yet another example of the new administration's "superlegalism," Obama's executive order called for the creation of a task force to make sure that renditions "do not result in the transfer of individuals to other nations to face torture" or otherwise circumvent human rights laws and treaties. This curious juridical caveat attached to the practice of international kidnapping was apparently sufficient to turn some former (rather vociferous) critics of rendition during the Bush regime to loyal supporters of rendition under Obama. As Tom Malinkowski, the Washington advocacy director for Human Rights Watch, declared in response to the new executive order: "Under limited circumstances, there is a legitimate place [for renditions]. What I heard loud and clear from the president's order was that they want to design a system that doesn't result in people being sent to foreign dungeons to be tortured."[11] If President Obama's imperialist legalism was predictable enough, HRW's about-face on rendition took many by surprise. The fact that liberal commentators are frequently taken aback by positions adopted by the large human rights organizations evidences the degree to which human rights is shrouded in an ahistorical set of assumptions that suppose human rights to have some kind of ideal (platonic) form not subject to the contingencies and vicissitudes of power, interests, and politics. Consequently liberal advocates for human rights continually find their jaws dropping whenever the discourse of human rights is demonstrably shown to be in-history.[12]

The selective revamping of U.S. imperialism poses a great deal of trouble for critics and scholars for whom international law has been repeatedly held up as the preferred progressive response to the imperialist unilateralism and brutal "excesses" of the Bush years. With the adoption of smart power and more careful attention paid to the *legalizability* of the "tools of counterterrorism," it appears that international law can once again reemerge as the preferred cloak of the neoimperial state — at least when and where the Law of the International can be made to align with U.S. (imperial) interests.[13] Despite the duplicities and contradictions of imperialist legalism, the discourse is designed to more effectively manage the field of perception ("the message we send to the world"), while keeping the only truly inflexible principle, the advancement of U.S. imperialist interests, in place.

The return of a smart and cool veneer to U.S. imperialism, likely to include considerable rhetorical genuflection to the "rule of international law" and the occasional multilateral offensive, may well bring certain liberal sectors back into the fold of U.S. imperialism, but it also effectively troubles *any* legalist strategy geared to denounce U.S. imperial actions abroad on the grounds that they are either "illegal" or "unilateral." The impending crisis for juridical-minded critics of U.S. imperialism resides in the fact that the Obama administration, like the Clinton regime of the 1990s, recognizes "that multilateralism can be just as, if not more, effective an imperial strategy as unilateralism."[14] Indeed, the unabashed human rights imperialist Nossel has no difficulty declaring that multilateralism should never rule over the new imperial calculus: "entrusting the liberal internationalist agenda to the multilateral system is neither viable nor sound."[15] Against this imperialist project of flexible power, dumb or smart, brutal or benign, we need to advance an anti-imperialist internationalism whose flexibilities emanate from recognition of the enormous multiplicity of people's needs and not from the minds of legal advisors whose task is to find ever new means of dissimulation. In this counterhegemonic project we need a more radical reckoning with what internationalist traditions from the International Workingmen's Association to the World Social Forum, and from Du Bois and Fanon to Alexander and Miéville, have long recognized: imperialist interests and international justice can never be reconciled.

Notes

Introduction

1. Proskauer to Du Bois, October 1944, *The Correspondence of W. E. B. Du Bois,* ed. Herbert Aptheker (Amherst: University of Massachusetts Press), 23.

2. Du Bois to Proskauer, November 1944, ibid., 24–25.

3. David L. Lewis, *W. E. B. Du Bois: The Fight for Equality and the American Century, 1919–1963* (New York: Macmillan, 2000), 503. As Lewis remarks, the "influential" Commission to Study the Organization of Peace included such notable persons as Roger Baldwin, John Foster Dulles, Merle Curti, Max Lerner, Owen Lattimore, Virginia Gildersleve, Philip Jessup, and Claude Pepper (503).

4. Ibid., 509.

5. William L. Patterson, ed., *We Charge Genocide: The Crime of Government against the Negro People* (New York: International Publishers, 1970). Since his initial formulation of the "problem of the color-line," Du Bois consistently cast the issue of racism in an international frame. As he wrote in 1903: "The problem of the twentieth century is the problem of the color-line, — the relation of the darker to the lighter races of men in Asia and Africa, in America and the islands of the sea." W. E. B. Du Bois, *The Souls of Black Folk* (New York: Bantam Books, 1989), 10.

6. Samir Amin recently advanced this concept of an internationalism of peoples in his important book *The World We Wish to See: Revolutionary Objectives in the Twenty-First Century,* trans. James Membrez (New York: Monthly Review Press, 2008). His genealogy of this anti-imperialist internationalism runs from the First International of 1864, called the International Workingmen's Association and "designed precisely to overcome the emergent separation [of working peoples] into national groupings" (11), to an emerging "Fifth International," which he says "should not be an assembly exclusively of political parties, but should gather all peoples' movements of resistance and struggle and guarantee both their voluntary participation in the construction of joint strategies and the independence of their own decision making" (79).

7. See, e.g., Marshall Berman, "Modernism and Human Rights near the Millennium," *Dissent* (Summer 1995), and Bruce Robbins, *Feeling Global: Internationalism in Distress* (New York: New York University Press, 1999).

8. See, e.g., David Harvey, *Spaces of Hope* (Berkeley, Calif.: University of California Press, 2000), and Marjorie Agosín, *A Map of Hope: Women's Writing on Human Rights–An International Literary Anthology* (New Brunswick, N.J.: Rutgers University Press, 2000).

9. See, e.g., Michael Hardt and Antonio Negri, *Empire* (Cambridge, Mass.: Harvard University Press, 2000).

10. To give but one example of the stark difference of opinion from within the metropolitan left consider the following two statements. The first from Arjun Appadurai: "While global capital and the system of nation-states negotiate the terms of the emergent world-order, a worldwide order of institutions has emerged that bears witness to what we may call 'grassroots globalization' or 'globalization from below.' The most easily recognizable of these institutions are NGOs (nongovernmental organizations) concerned with mobilizing highly specific local, national, and regional groups on matters of equity, access, justice and redistribution. These organizations have complex relations with the state, with the official public sphere, with international civil society initiatives, and with local communities. Sometimes they are uncomfortably complicit with the policies of the nation-state and sometimes they are violently opposed to these policies. Sometimes they have grown wealthy and powerful enough to constitute major political forces in their own right and sometimes they are weak in everything except their transparency and local legitimacy. NGOs have their roots in the progressive movements of the last two centuries in the areas of labor, suffrage, and civil rights. They sometimes have historical links to socialist internationalism of an earlier era.... Although the sociology of these emergent social forms — part movements, part networks, part organizations — has yet to be developed, there is considerable progressive consensus that these forms are the crucibles and institutional instruments of most serious efforts to globalize from below." Arjun Appadurai, "Grassroots Globalization and the Research Imagination," *Public Culture* 12, no. 1 (2000): 15. In contradistinction to Appadurai's formulation of "populism from below," Michael Hardt and Antonio Negri cast international human rights activism as a form of high moral imperialism in the service of Empire: "The Empire's powers of intervention might be best understood as beginning not directly with its weapons of lethal force but rather with its moral instruments. What we are calling moral intervention is practiced today by a variety of bodies ... but the most important may be some of the so-called nongovernmental organizations, which, precisely because they are not run directly by governments, are assumed to act on the basis of ethical or moral imperatives. The term refers to a wide variety of groups, but

we are referring here principally to the global, regional and local organizations that are dedicated to relief work and the protection of human rights, such as Amnesty International, Oxfam, and Médecins sans Frontières. Such humanitarian NGOs are in effect (even if this runs counter to the intentions of the participants) some of the most powerful pacific weapons of the New World Order — the charitable campaigns and the mendicant orders of Empire. These NGOs conduct 'just wars' without arms, without violence, without borders." Hardt and Negri, *Empire*, 35–36.

11. Universal Declaration of Human Rights, Article 2. The enumerated rights included: the right to life, liberty and the security of the person; to recognition as a person before the law; to equal protection before the law; to effective remedy; to be presumed innocent; to freedom of movement... within the borders; to leave any country, including his own, and to return to his country; to seek and to enjoy in other countries asylum from persecution; to a nationality; to marry [men and women of full age]; to own property; to freedom of thought, conscience and religion; to freedom of opinion and expression; to freedom of peaceful assembly and association; to take part in the Government of his country; to social security; to work; to equal pay for equal work; to just and favourable renumeration insuring for himself and his family an existence worthy of human dignity; to form and join trade unions; to rest and leisure, including reasonable limitation of working hours and periodic holidays with pay; to a standard of living adequate for health and well-being of himself and of his family, including food, clothing, housing, and medical care and necessary social services, ...to security in the event of unemployment, sickness, disability, widowhood, old age or other lack of livelihood; to education; to participate in the cultural life of the community, to enjoy the arts and to share in scientific advancement and its benefits; to the protection of the moral and material interests resulting from any scientific, literary or artistic production of which he is the author. (UDHR, Articles 3–27) Quite an impressive litany indeed.

12. Jacques Derrida, *Specters of Marx: The State of the Debt, the Work of Mourning and the New International*, trans. Peggy Kamuf (New York: Routledge, 1994), 85

13. Ibid., 85.

14. Karl Marx and Friedrich Engels, *Manifesto of the Communist Party* (New York: International Publishers, 1948), 8.

15. The UDHR was ratified 48–0 with 8 other nations from the Soviet bloc abstaining.

16. The specter of communism evoked by Marx and Engels was a collective figure, despite the singularity of the name given to those diverse revolutionary movements spreading across Europe in the mid-nineteenth century. And further, as Jacques Derrida has suggestively argued, Marx's own ghostly rhetorical figures were decidedly plural. See Derrida, *Specters*

of Marx. The reference to a "many-headed hydra" is drawn from the exceptional work of Peter Linebaugh and Marcus Rediker, *The Many-Headed Hydra: Sailors, Slaves, Commoners, and the Hidden History of the Revolutionary Atlantic* (Boston: Beacon Press, 2000).

17. As the historian Rita Maran writes, "international horror at the holocaust was a principal stimulus to the creation of human rights safeguards by the United Nations." Rita Maran, *Torture: The Role of Ideology in the French-Algerian War* (New York: Praeger, 1989), 7.

18. More commonly, the Nazi Holocaust was conceived as the unimaginable event, as that which could not happen but did happen in the self-proclaimed lands of civility and civilization — a failure of the Enlightenment writ large across those nations and powers, old and new, for which the vaunted rights of man and the citizen, tied as they were to the nation-state form, no longer served as an adequate mode of protection. For a brilliant critique of this historicization and its baleful elisions of colonial violence, see Aimé Césaire, *Discourse on Colonialism,* trans. Joan Pinkham (New York: Monthly Review Press, 2000).

19. In his recent account of "international law from below," Balakrishnan Rajagopal argues cogently that "international law and the Third World are like Siamese twins: one can not even imagine them as separate from one another because development, human rights, environmental, and other institutions operate mostly in the third world." According to Rajagopal, the colonial native made its explicit inaugural appearance in the text of international law with the invention of the Mandate system in the League of Nations. The Mandate distinguished three sets of "interests" that must be born in mind by the League's Commission: international interests, national interests, and "native interests." The latter interest, according to organizers, was central "since the promotion of the welfare of the Mandated Territories is the primary object"(39). And in its centrality, Rajagopal argues, we can discern "how international institutions [since the Mandate system] played the crucial mediating role in the transition between colonialism and development and, in that process, *helped manage mass resistance*" (53, emphasis added). So while the explicit evocation of the native may have been absent from the text of the documents of the Second World War international, it was not because the "interests of the native" were no longer a primary object of concern or regulation, but rather because the natives' demands (in their dense singularities) had outpaced the victors' capacity to discursively fix them in place as an object of control. Instead they were unceremoniously handed over to the formalism of a new universality. Balakrishnan Rajagopal, *International Law from Below: Development, Social Movements, and Third World Resistance* (Cambridge: Cambridge University Press, 2003).

20. Samir Amin, *Beyond U.S. Hegemony? Assessing the Prospects for a Multipolar World,* trans. Patrick Camiller (New York: Zed Books, 2006),

8. The initial phase of the global deployment of capitalism was, according to Amin, "impeded until the collapse of the post-war social orders (welfare state, Sovietism, national populism in the South)" (8). Since this time, roughly the end of the Cold War, the United States has moved to seize greater and greater control over this "triad," a strategy that threatens to disorganize the hitherto effective imperial collectivity.

21. Aijaz Ahmad, *In Theory: Classes, Nations, Literatures* (London: Verso Books, 1992), 22.

22. Amin, *Beyond U.S. Hegemony?* 12. To which he correctly adds, "The aim of this strategy is neither to ensure open markets for all (which exist only in the propaganda of neoliberal sycophants) nor, of course, to make democracy prevail throughout the world" (12–13).

23. China Miéville, *Between Equal Rights: A Marxist Theory of International Law* (Chicago: Haymarket Books, 2005), 293. The full passage for this claim reads as follows: "The international legal form assumes juridical equality and unequal violence of sovereign states. In the context of modern international capitalism, that unequal violence is imperialism itself. The necessity of this unequal violence derives precisely from the juridical equality: one of the legal subjects makes law out of the legal relation by means of their coercive power — their imperialist domination. Specifically in its universalized form, predicated on juridical equality and self-determination, international law assumes imperialism."

24. Derrida, *Spectres of Marx*, 83–84.

25. I do not mean to suggest that there are not quite useful analyses of transnational networks coming out of various disciplinary locations; however, the general assumption that there are no longer any political alternatives to contemporary processes of globalization has cleared the way for a conception of global civil society that is, at best, hopelessly idealized and, at worst, fully complicit with neoliberal structures of domination.

26. Nelson Mandela, "The Rivonia Trial," *No Easy Walk to Freedom: In His Own Words* (London: Heinemann, 1965), 168.

27. The concept of the "Gay International" comes from Joseph Massad in "Re-Orienting Desire: The Gay International and the Arab World," *Public Culture* 14, no. 2 (2002): 361–85. In Massad's formulation, the "Gay International" is an ideological formation comprised of a set of missionary tasks (universalize gay rights), a discourse that produces gays and lesbians around the world, and organizations that carry forth the political agenda, such as the International Lesbian and Gay Association and the International Lesbian and Gay Human Rights Commission.

28. In the case of the communications industries, as Hardt and Negri point out, "What the theories of power of modernity were forced to consider transcendent, that is external to productive and social relations, is here formed inside, immanent to the productive and social relations. Mediation is absorbed within the productive machine. The political synthesis of social

space is fixed in the space of communication. This is why communications have assumed such a central position." Moreover, "communicative production and the construction of imperial legitimation march hand in hand and can no longer be separated." Hardt and Negri, *Empire*, 33–34.

29. Ibid., 36.

30. The Sandinistas and their allies throughout Latin America like to say that Somoza was *ajusticiado*, literally, brought to justice. For a very funny but brief account of Somoza and *ajusticiado*, see María Josefina Saldaña Portillo's entry on "Somoza" in *Sissy: The Lexicon* published as a supplementary guidebook for the world premiere of Ricardo Bracho's brilliant play, "Sissy" (Company of Angels, Los Angeles, June 2008). For her more extensive account of revolutionary politics in Latin America, see Saldaña-Portillo's, *The Revolutionary Imagination in the Americas and the Age of Development* (Durham, N.C.: Duke University Press, 2003).

31. On the concept of the nonconvertibility of violence, see Étienne Balibar, "Violence, Ideality, and Cruelty," in *Politics and the Other Scene*, trans. Christine Jones, James Swenson, and Chris Turner (London: Verso, 2002).

32. Balibar, *Politics and the Other Scene*, xi–xii.

33. On the long history of this modern democratic exchange and the central role of culture, see David Lloyd and Paul Thomas's *Culture and the State* (New York: Routledge, 1998).

34. In other words, political struggle always takes place within conditions of unequal force, and any revolutionary praxis must attempt to anticipate and prepare for the transformation of oppositional forms into regressive forms before or after the realization of their revolutionary ends. This historic problem of convertibility is not "solved" however, simply by rejecting the strategic appropriation of dominant forms — in any case, an impossibility (the romanticized mythologies of Gandhi and King notwithstanding).

35. As China Miéville writes, "on occasions, such as *Nicaragua vs. US*, a ruling may be given against the imperialist action of a powerful state. . . . [However] the system that throws these problems up *is* the juridical system that underpins the law. Law is a relation between subjects abstracted of social context. . . . Internationally, law's 'violence of abstraction' *is* the violence of war. To fundamentally change the dynamics of the system it would be necessary not to reform the institutions but to *eradicate the forms of law* — which means the fundamental reformulation of the political-economic system of which they are expressions. The project to achieve this is the best hope for global emancipation, and it would mean the end of law." Mieville, *Between Equal Rights*, 317–18.

36. In addition to the theorists mentioned, who are specifically named because I deal with their work directly in chapter 5 of this book, a longer but still *very* partial list of those who currently offer critiques of international structures of governance in an anticolonial mode would include Samir

Amin, Sandra Angeleri, Étienne Balibar, Atilio Boron, Enrique Dussel, Nasser Hussein, David Lloyd, Lisa Lowe, Achille Mbembe, Balakrishnan Rajagopal, and Lisa Yoneyama. As with any such hopelessly partial list, I offer my apologies to the many out there with whom I am either not familiar or whom I've failed to mention, but who deserve to be recognized among this grouping.

37. This tripartite mapping of contemporary state formations is taken from the recent work of M. Jacqui Alexander. In her analysis of the transnational present, Alexander describes the neocolonial state formation as made up of "those states that emerged from the colonial 'order' as the forfeiters to nationalist claims to sovereignty and autonomy," and the neo-imperial state form as comprised of "those advanced capitalist states that are the dominant partners in the global 'order'" (4). What is most interesting about her mapping of contemporary state formations is that she rejects locating these forms as operating in discrete blocs (colonialism here, neocolonialism there, and so on) and in placing them in a linear temporality (*from* the backward colonial *to* the advanced neoimperial); instead she attempts to grasp their operations "in different places at the same time, and also in the same place at the same time" (182). M. Jacqui Alexander, *Pedagogies of Crossing: Meditations on Feminism, Sexual Politics, Memory, and the Sacred* (Durham, N.C.: Duke University Press, 2005).

38. "The Bamako Appeal" is reprinted in Amin, *The World We Wish to See*, 111.

39. Peter Beaumont and agencies, "Israel May Face War Crimes Trials ver Gaza," *Guardian* (UK), March 2, 2009. The ICC, with its 108 members, has neither recognized Palestine as a sovereign state nor as a member, but under mounting pressure behind this case to do something, the ICC has moved to adduce whether the Palestinian Authority operates enough like a state, and is regarded by others as a state, in order to bring the case before the court.

40. The International Criminal Court was established in 2002 with a mandate to "investigate and prosecute genocide, crimes against humanity, and war crimes." Israel, like the United States, signed onto the treaty establishing the ICC, but neither government submitted it to their respective representative bodies for full ratification. Without complete ratification, the findings of the court remain nonbinding for these signatory countries. In the case of the United States, President Bush "unsigned" the agreement in May 2002 after Clinton signed onto it in 2000. President Obama has been fairly quiet on the matter since his election, having previously taken a "wait-and-see" attitude until it could be determined that the ICC will operate in such a way "that reflects American sovereignty and promotes our national security interests." Response to candidate questionnaire, 2004.

41. "Barrier Ruling Shifts the Debate," *Guardian* (UK), July 10, 2004. Furthermore, as China Miéville has pointed out, Palestinian negotiators are

reluctant to press entities like the UN Security Council for expressions of support for reasons of *realpolitik.* As one negotiator pointed out, "It would [merely] highlight America's role as a friend of Israel, and I'm not sure the Palestinians actually want to isolate the Americans." Miéville, *Between Equal Rights,* 298.

42. Benjamin Rutland, spokesman for the Israeli military, "Demands Grow for Gaza War Crimes Investigation," *Guardian* (UK), January 13, 2009.

43. There are a few notable exceptions with which I am familiar, although there may well be more, and they can be found in the recent work of China Miéville, *Between Equal Rights: A Marxist Theory of International Law* (Chicago: Haymarket Books, 2006), and Danilo Zolo, *Cosmopolis: Prospects for World Government* (Cambridge: Polity Press, 1997). More on both of these works in chapter 5.

44. Miéville, *Between Equal Rights,* esp. 225–93.

45. As the influential human rights advocate Samantha Power puts it, we must "believe in international law." www.salon.com/news/feature/2008_02_18/samantha_power/index1.html. (This claim will be discussed in detail in chapter 5).

46. This is analogous to the starting point suggested by Peter Linebaugh in his analysis of crime and criminality in *The London Hanged: Crime and Civil Society in the Eighteenth Century* (Cambridge: Cambridge University Press, 1992). This is *not* to say, however, as Judith Butler recently argues, that our starting point should be built around a politics of mourning. In *Precarious Life,* Butler says that after 9/11 "loss has made a tenuous 'we' of us all" and that this can serve as the basis for the articulation of a new politics of community. As Lisa Lowe argues, while "grief may permit reckoning with war and historical violence, and move us from individualized mourning to projects of collective war memories, social movements for redress and reparations or public campaigns for the prosecution of war crimes, . . . [such a] politics of human vulnerability risks engaging a universalism that commits violence anew, reiterating and appropriating divisions as it makes claim to grief." This danger is demonstrably evident in Butler's formulation with its uncritical reliance upon the exceptionalist discourse of "9/11" as historical event zero. Lisa Lowe, "An Ethics of Reckoning," talk delivered at University of California–Riverside, December 2008. The Butler quotation cited above is from Judith Butler, *Precarious Life: The Powers of Mourning and Violence* (New York: Verso Press, 2004), 20. And for an excellent account of the contemporary limits of a discourse of redress, Lisa Yoneyama argues that a politics of redressive justice must contend, in a grossly unequal battle, with the increasing *Americanization* of the post–Cold War International. As she writes: "By restating globalization and transnationalization as "Americanization," I wish to underscore that, rather than mitigating the nation-state formation, the globalization of the

political economy and militarism has in fact buttressed the hegemony of the United States as an imperial nation, both across the globe and over its own residents and citizens." Lisa Yoneyama, "Traveling Memories, Contagious Justice: Americanization of Japanese War Crimes at the End of the Post–Cold War," *Journal of Asian American Studies* (February 2003): 60.

1. Conscience Denied

1. Peter Benenson, "The Forgotten Prisoners," *Observer* (London), May 28, 1961.

2. Figures are from Amnesty International's Annual Report of 2005, www.amnesty.org.

3. Edward Said, "Nationalism, Human Rights, and Interpretation," *Raritan* 12, no. 3 (Winter 1993): 55.

4. Edy Kaufman, "Prisoners of Conscience: The Shaping of a New Human Rights Concept," *Human Rights Quarterly* 13 (1991): 340.

5. Benenson, "The Forgotten Prisoners."

6. The first systematic account of the category of the political prisoner can be found in George Sigerson's 1890 publication, *Political Prisoners at Home and Abroad* (London: Kegan Paul, Trench, Trübner & Co, 1890). More recently, Irish historian Seán McConville has located the origins of the figure of the political prisoner around 1848, when the question of political detention, and the potential for turning imprisonment to the prisoner's advantage, troubled several European governments in the aftermath of revolution. The political prisoners that McConville discusses were not pacifists, but militants who opposed British rule through the use of force. See McConville, *Irish Political Prisoners 1848–1922: Theatres of War* (London: Routledge, 2003).

7. For an account of the origins of Amnesty International, see Egon Larsen, *A Flame in Barbed Wire: The Story of Amnesty International* (New York: W. W. Norton, 1979).

8. All descriptions come from Benenson's, "The Forgotten Prisoners."

9. For an account of Mandela's imprisonment, see Nelson Mandela, in *No Easy Walk to Freedom: In His Own Words* (London: Heinemann, 1965).

10. Nelson Mandela, "The Rivonia Trial," *No Easy Walk to Freedom*, 168.

11. Ibid., 163.

12. *Umkhonto we Sizwe* translates as "The Spear of the Nation." Mandela was commander-in-chief of Umkhonto.

13. Mandela, "The Rivonia Trial," 164.

14. As Michel Foucault has noted and as is applicable to this trial: "political trials are always touchstones. Not because the accused are never criminals, but because public authority shows itself without a mask, and presents itself for judgment in judging its enemies." Foucault,

Power/Knowledge: Selected Interviews and Other Writings 1972–1977, ed. Colin Gordon (New York: Pantheon Books, 1980), 441. Mandela's admission of guilt serves as an attempt to displace the question of the accused's [his and his fellow comrades'] guilt or innocence before the law and shift the focus of the trial to examine the legitimacy of the law/state *to pass judgment* on either criminality or morality.

15. Mandela, "The Rivonia Trial," 165.

16. Steve Mufson, *Fighting Years: Black Resistance and the Struggle for a New South Africa* (Boston: Beacon Press, 1990), 96.

17. Mandela, "The Rivonia Trial," 166.

18. For an account of the vote that was publicly announced and discussed at the Amnesty International meeting in Canterbury (September 1964), see Larsen, *A Flame in Barbed Wire*, 24–25.

19. The concept of violence does play a significant role in understanding the divergence between Amnesty's human rights politics and the ANC's decolonization politics; however, my point here is that this difference is inadequately posed in the abstract terms of violence/nonviolence. How the place of violence *should* be understood is the subject of the remaining pages of this chapter.

20. As Mandela argued in his statement from the dock, Umkhonto was formed in part because the ANC was committed to nonviolence. Members who had joined the ANC had joined an organization that was expressly nonviolent; therefore, according to Mandela, either the question of violence had to be put before the entire organization (an impractical option), or another organization should be formed. The ANC, along with affinity organizations, including the Communist Party, opted to form a new organization, Umkhonto.

21. Kaufman, "Prisoners of Conscience," 350.

22. Neil Belton, *The Good Listener, Helen Bamber: A Life against Cruelty* (New York: Pantheon Books, 1999), 160.

23. In the words of Bamber's biographer, Neil Belton, "this was not a politics: it was a drawing of boundaries for any political action." Belton, *The Good Listener, Helen Bamber,* 180.

24. Peter Benenson, "Are Human Rights Universal?" *Commentary* 64, no. 3 (1977): 60–63.

25. Raymond Williams, *Keywords: A Vocabulary of Culture and Society,* rev. ed. (Oxford: Oxford University Press, 1983), 77.

26. For an extensive list of Amnesty's organizational principles, see www.amnesty.org.

27. Peter R. Baehr, *Human Rights: Universality in Practice* (New York: Palgrave Macmillan, 2001), 116.

28. Mandela, "A Land Ruled by the Gun," *No Easy Walk to Freedom,* 110.

29. Mandela, "No Easy Walk to Freedom," 27.

30. Mandela, "The Rivonia Trial," 175.

31. Frantz Fanon, *Wretched of the Earth,* trans. Richard Philcox (New York: Grove Press, 2004), 2.

32. Belton, *The Good Listener, Helen Bamber,* 180.

33. Fanon, *Wretched of the Earth,* 23.

34. The concept of "illegal laws" was introduced in the 1980s by Amnesty to allow for nonviolent forms of resistance that were expressly illegal under the laws of a state but could nevertheless be clearly considered just. The "last resort clause" was also introduced in the late 1980s to allow for forms of *violent* resistance that involved "minimal damage to either persons or property after all other forms of protest had been tried and exhausted." Kaufman, "Prisoners of Conscience," 346.

35. Richard Falk, *Predatory Globalization: A Critique* (Cambridge: Polity Press, 1999), 98.

36. In a telling dismissal of historical critiques of Amnesty's disqualification of Mandela, one of Amnesty's board of directors, Morton Winston, claimed in 1994 that the issue should be laid to rest: "So those of you who would like to raise this old chestnut again would do better to think twice about doing so. Wouldn't it be wiser to devote our attention to the world's current spate of human rights violations?" Yet another striking example of the deeply antihistorical thrust that animates far too much of human rights activist practice. www.africa.upenn.edu.

37. Michel Foucault as cited in Keith Ansell-Pearson, *An Introduction to Nietzsche as Political Thinker* (Cambridge: Cambridge University Press, 1994), 174.

38. Wendy Brown, *States of Injury: Power and Freedom in Late Modernity* (Princeton, N.J.: Princeton University Press, 1995), 97.

39. Said, "Nationalism, Human Rights, and Interpretation," 16.

40. The Peace of Westphalia (1648) marked the beginning of the modern system of nation-states. And although it is nominally in disrepute as having ushered in a protracted period of competition between nation-states, there is little to suggest that such a period has come to a close with the rise of either more cooperative supranational structures or an international civil society. Subsequent chapters will have much more to say on the increased willingness of states to sign on to the principles of international human rights.

41. Rearticulated after the "events of 9/11" in the immortal words of President George Bush as "you are either with us or against us," whereby exclusions cast one as a member of the "axis of evil." I say here *relatively* inexpensive because the currency of human rights on the global market is considerably lower than the opening of markets to capitalist penetration, the privatization of key industries and public goods, and the restructuring of government expenditures away from any significant redistribution of wealth toward the poor. In this way, nations are not going

to be rejected if they refuse the human rights aspects of the deal; however, they will be cut out and subject to isolation and/or overthrow if they refuse the economic aspects of the new world order. Nevertheless, the human rights components are increasing in value, insofar as the hegemons of the global economy have begun to find them more and more useful as evidenced by the recent comments of the U.S. State Department: "Today, all the talk is of globalization. But far too often, both its advocates and its critics have portrayed globalization as an exclusively economic and technological phenomenon. In fact, in the new millennium, there are at least three universal 'languages': money, the Internet, and democracy and human rights. An overlooked 'third globalization' — the rise of transnational human rights networks of both public and private actors — has helped develop what may over time become an international civil society capable of working with governments, international institutions, and multinational corporations to promote both democracy and the standards embodied in the Universal Declaration of Human Rights" (U.S. State Department, "The Third Globalization: Transnational Human Rights Networks," www.state.gov/www/global/human_rights/1999_hrp_report/overview.html.)

42. David Lloyd, *Anomalous States: Irish Writing and the Post-Colonial Moment* (Durham, N.C.: Duke University Press, 1993), 236. Historian Charles Tilly has also detailed this coming into being for modern European nation-states with his account of the history of demilitarization and the subsequent monopoly over the means of violence by the new centralized nation-state. See Charles Tilly "State Making and War Making as Organized Crime," in *Bringing the State Back In,* ed. Peter Evans et al (Cambridge: Cambridge University Press, 1985).

43. Nicos Poulantzas, *State, Power, Socialism* (London: Verso Books, 2001), 46.

44. I have emphasized the critical role which the Law plays in the hegemonic process of convertibility, but other public institutions like schools also play an absolutely indispensable role in the production of ideological subjects for whom the legitimacy of the institutions of the state becomes a given. In particular, the educational apparatus is charged with (re)producing a historical narrative that naturalizes the violence of the nation as both an extension of the institution of the Law and as the law of progress, from its originary monopolization to the present and beyond.

45. The prolix traffic between techniques of colonial repression and metropolitan repression is the subject of my essay, "A State of Permanent Exception: The Birth of Modern Policing in Colonial Capitalism," *Interventions: Journal of Post-Colonial Studies* 5, no. 3 (August 2003): 322–44.

46. Michel Foucault, "The Ethic of Care for the Self as a Practice of Freedom: An Interview with Michel Foucault on January 20, 1984," *The Final*

Foucault, ed. James Bernauer and David Rasmussen (Cambridge, Mass.: MIT Press, 1988), 20.

47. Quotation from Pablo Neruda in January 1970. The full quote from Neruda reads: "You cannot say, 'I don't believe in violence as a general political axiom.' "

48. It is important to note here that there is little in the ANC's approach to violence or Mandela's conceptualization of it that affirms Fanon's notion of violence as a "cleansing force." As Fanon once wrote, "violence is a cleansing force. It frees the native from his inferiority complex and from his despair and inaction; it makes him fearless and restores his self-respect" (*Wretched of the Earth,* 51). For Mandela, contra Fanon, the use of violence was conceived mainly as a last resort to bring whites "to their senses." Any transformative effects such actions might have on the colonized subject fell outside the scope of strategic calculation.

49. The Black People's Convention (BPC) was founded in 1972 and came to serve as the umbrella organization for some seventy different black consciousness groups and associations, such as the South African Students Movement (SASM), the National Association of Youth Organizations (NAYO) and the Black Workers Project (BWP).

50. Mufson, *Fighting Years,* 196.

51. According to Mufson, many militants dismissed Tutu's position claiming that "Tutu is an international figure. He has to be seen to be non-violent. But ordinary youths are not apologists for the dictates of the international community' "(99).

52. To which Tutu immediately added that "if [he] were a young black, [he] wouldn't follow a man named Bishop Tutu." Mufson, *Fighting Years,* 103.

2. Who Claims Modernity?

1. In 1991, some thirteen years later, Amnesty International did take up the issue of sexuality, making the human rights of lesbians and gays part of its mandate.

2. The ILGA's consultative status was, however, revoked less than a year later when opponents, led by North Carolina senator Jesse Helms, charged the group with promoting pedophilia. ILGA's members included NAMBLA (the North American Man–Boy Love Association) and this was enough for a majority of UN member states to vote to withdraw ILGA's consultative status.

3. Massad, "Re-Orienting Desire," 361–85.

4. The juridical turn in gay politics can be distinguished from the politics of sexuality predominant in the 1970s when, according to Lisa Duggan, "gay liberation exploded onto a rapidly shifting scene of contest over the meanings of public and private, and the related meanings of democracy and autonomy in collective and personal life. Following the 1969 Stonewall

rebellion and the subsequent emergence of new organizations and rhetorics, gay politics began to interact intensely with feminist, countercultural, and antiracist rhetorics and strategies." The legalistic turn in U.S. gay and lesbian politics "provided incentives for litigation organizations...and strengthened the appeal of human rights as the dominant public demand of the movement." Lisa Duggan, *The Twilight of Equality? Neoliberalism, Cultural Politics, and the Attack on Democracy* (New York: Beacon Press, 2003), 52–53.

5. Neville Hoad, *African Intimacies: Race, Homosexuality, and Globalization* (Minneapolis: University of Minnesota Press, 2007), 60.

6. From the Founding Statement of the Gay Liberation Front (1969), cited in Colin Wilson, *Socialists and Gay Liberation* (London: Socialist Workers Party, UK 199–), 20.

7. Hoad, *African Intimacies,* 61.

8. In June 1994, three months after the García decision, Attorney General Janet Reno announced that sexual orientation would be classified as a social group eligible for asylum status under U.S. immigration law. This administrative decision would make it easier for sexual asylees to meet the criteria of persecution which mandate that such persecution must be "on account of race, religion, nationality, political opinion, or membership in a particular social group." The García case was not, however, the first of its kind, nor was it the precedent for Reno's announcement. As far back as 1990 the Board of Immigration Appeal (BIA) had approved asylum cases on the grounds of homosexual persecution. Such decisions remain in most instances confidential. According to Joseph Langlois, director of the INS-NY asylum office, "the confidentiality of these proceedings enables adjudicators to avoid concerns regarding foreign affairs implications since determinations on international human rights standards would be shielded from the applicants' foreign state." Phone interview with Langlois conducted by the author in July 1997. For more on asylum law, see note 12 below.

9. ILGHRC and ILGA, joint press release March 22, 1994.

10. Covarrubias in conversation with the International Lesbian and Gay Human Rights Commission, program director for the region of Latin America, Jorge Cortiñas. Recounted to the author by Cortiñas on the same day in mid-1993.

11. Comment from Julie Dorf, executive director of ILGHRC, to Jorge Cortiñas.

12. Chandan Reddy has recently written a superb analysis of the issue of sexual asylum cases and narratives with respect to homosexuality. He locates asylum law within the United States as bound more to "international human rights" than to U.S. domestic, or even INS, law. As Reddy writes: "While asylum law within the U.S. is under the authority of the INS, the judges who preside over the administrative cases are generally

understood as exempt from some of the mandates of national immigration law that otherwise define admission into the U.S. Instead, these judges are bound to broadly defined 'international human rights' standards as established by the UN Declaration of Rights for Refugees, Exiles and Persecuted Social Groups.... In this way, asylum cases represent 'anomalous states' from the perspective of national right, marking instead the emergence of supposedly new capitalist social formations that are parasitical of the modern institutions of the state and its forms of power." Chandan Reddy, "Asian Diasporas, Neoliberalism, and Family: Reviewing the Case for Homosexual Asylum in the Context of Family Rights," *Social Text* (Fall–Winter 2005): 102.

13. George Yúdice, "We Are Not the World," *Social Text,* nos. 31–32 (1992): 203.

14. In ILGHRC's press release dated May 8, 1994, they say that "at least 15, and possibly as many as 25, transvestites and gay men were assassinated in Tuxtla Gutiérrez." In late 1994, Amnesty International says "at least 11 gay men were killed" during the same period of time, with four other murders whose relatedness was contested by the police.

15. "Psicosis en Chiapas por la cacería de homosexuales," *Proceso* 852 (March 1, 1993): 26.

16. For an insightful account on narrative techniques of state disavowal, see Rosa Linda Fregoso's essay "Toward a Planetary Civil Society," in *MeXicana Encounters: The Making of Social Identities on the Borderlands* (Berkeley: University of California Press, 2003), 1–29. In this essay Fregoso tracks attempts by the state of Chihuahua to cover over their ineptitude and/or complicity with the recent long history of murders of women in the Ciudad Juárez area (some four hundred women have been killed and many more disappeared since 1993). According to Fregoso as it applies to these murders, the state's first technique was that of negation, by which public officials refused "to acknowledge the reality of systemic and calculated acts of violence against women" (3). When this ideological form of disavowal could no longer be held up, the state shifted to a second technique which Fregoso calls "disaggregation." Within this narrative framework, the state acknowledged that there were murders taking place, but "refused to accept their interconnection" (5). Many of the representational techniques used by various agencies and organizations, which Fregoso identifies as operative around the murders in Juarez, were also at work around the murders of the *travestis* in Chiapas — especially the media and police technique of raising the specter of prostitution and provocative dressing as a way of devaluing the victims or implying that they were somehow responsible for their own murders.

17. Cited in "Psicosis en Chiapas por la cacería de homosexuales," *Proceso* 852 (March 1, 1993): 25. Later, in January 1993, Governor González

Garrido would be named "Secretary of Government," the second most powerful federal post after the presidency by President Carlos Salinas.

18. Victor Ronquillo, *La muerte viste de rosa: Chiapas — La cacería de los travestis* (Mexico City: Ediciones Roca, 1994), 79.

19. Anonymous *travesti* cited in Pedro Bustos-Aguilar's, "Learning to Spell Chiapas," *Third Force* (May–June 1994): 12.

20. Teresa Jardí, "Action Letter from the Department of Human Rights of the Archdiocese of Mexico City," February 13, 1993.

21. Amnesty International's report of 1994 did, however, suggest that "the killing in May 1994 of another man [was] consistent with the pattern of killings of gays." Amnesty International, "Killings of Gay Men in Chiapas: The Impunity Continues," 1994.

22. Ronquillo, *La muerte viste de rosa*, 54.

23. Amnesty International, "Killings of Gay Men in Chiapas."

24. Bustos-Aguilar, "Learning to Spell Chiapas," 13.

25. *Travesti* and transgender groups frequently object to the equating of *travestis* and gays, arguing that these social identities are dissimilar enough to warrant distinction. Moreover, many transgender activists contend that transgenders face forms of persecution and oppression that gays and lesbians do not face. The movement of the *travesti* murders from ignored to backdrop would seem to corroborate the claim that these social identities are not equivalent.

26. I recite the names of those murdered here, because it was the specificity of these names and these lives that was denied entry and then symbolically aggregated at the moment of reification within international human rights discourse. At the same time, as Gayatri Spivak points out: "No perspective critical of imperialism can turn the Other into a self, because the project of imperialism has always already historically refracted what might have been the absolutely Other into a domesticated Other that consolidates the imperialist self." Spivak, "Three Women's Texts and a Critique of Imperialism," *Critical Inquiry* 12, no. 1 (1985): 253.

27. As Martin Manalansan has argued in a cogent critique of contemporary North American gay and lesbian discourse: "The globalization of gay and lesbian oppression obfuscates hierarchical relations between metropolitan centers and suburban peripheries.... [And] practices that do not conform with Western narratives of the development of individual political subjects are dismissed as unliberated or coded as 'homophobic.'" He attributes this to the fact that "the 'internationalizing' transnational gay and lesbian movement does not as yet contain a critique of its own universalizing categories; without an interrogation of its Eurocentric and bourgeois assumptions, this globalizing discourse risks duplicating an imperial gaze in relation to non-Western nonmetropolitan sexual practices and collectivities. Martin Manalansan IV, "In the Shadows of Stonewall: Examining Gay Transnational Politics and the Diasporic Dilemma," in *The Politics of*

Culture in the Shadow of Capital, ed. Lisa Lowe and David Lloyd (Durham, N.C.: Duke University Press, 1997), 486, 488.

28. The claim to immediacy typically constitutes a disavowal of mediation and thus functions as an alibi to continue trafficking in the same unexamined, but sanctioned, manner.

29. The "coming out" narrative serves as the basis for such an identity politic insofar as coming out is presumed to be the basis upon which the liberation of the subject is conditioned.

30. Barbara Harlow, "'All that is Inside Is Not Center': Responses to Discourses of Domination," in *Coming to Terms: Feminism, Theory, Politics,* ed. Elizabeth Weed (New York: Routledge, 1989), 162.

31. Quoted in Hermann Bellinghausen, "There Is a Great Effervescence of Social Movements That See Nothing for Them Up Above," *La Jornada* (February 5, 2006).

32. Subcomandante Marcos, "The Punch Card and the Hourglass," interview by Gabriel García Márquez and Roberto Pombo, *New Left Review* 9 (May–June 2001): 71.

33. Raul Zibechi, "Sex and Revolution," trans. Nalina Eggert, *Counterpunch* (December 21, 2007).www.counterpunch.org/zibechi12212007.html.

34. For those looking for alternatives to sex work, there are other productive projects, involving handicrafts, production and sale of clothing, and working at the condom stores. In order to try to create more nonexploitative working conditions, the members of the network form cooperatives in order to share resources and avoid dependence on either the state or informal and exploitative prostitution rings. The first cooperative was established by a group of transvestites who called themselves the Angeles en Busca de Libertad (Angels Searching for Freedom). One of the most successful enterprises of the Network are the two clinics that the sex workers run in Mexico City. In contrast to the state-run clinics notorious for their corruption and discriminatory treatment toward sex workers, the sex-worker-run clinics are self-managed and provide services free of charge. The bulk of the funding for the clinics (some 85 percent) comes from "social condom marketing" whereby condoms are sold at different prices depending on the ability of the buyer. No one at the clinic is salaried, and the only people who are paid for their work are the doctors. In 2004 the members of the Street Brigade came into contact with the Colectivo de Salud para Todos y Todas, comprised of university students who coordinate health projects in the autonomous Zapatista communities. Their coming together generated the 270-page manual entitled "La otra campaña de salud sexual y reproductiva para la resistencia indígena y campesina en México."

35. The divide is not, as is frequently supposed, between state-centered and non-state-centered movements (nor between indigenous and non-indigenous-based revolutionary organizations), but rather the differences between popular struggles should be understood by the degree to which

grassroots forces *from below* direct and determine structures of governance from above. In contexts where popular movements succeed in seizing state structures (as in Bolivia and Venezuela), the popular-state dialectic must be differently negotiated than in, say, contemporary Mexico. Different, but not necessarily opposed. As Marcos says about the relation between the Zapatistas and other emergent forms of popular struggle: "we are interested in this idea of proposing a new path, one that isn't just leftist in its rhetoric, but one that comes out against capitalism.... We don't want to tell anyone what to do; we want them to tell us; but it has to come from those at the bottom. We don't want to hear what Evo Morales has to say about Bolivia, but instead what the indigenous who rose up have to say, what the people who are in struggle in Brazil, in Argentina, everywhere ... what those at the bottom have to say. And in the case of Venezuela, same thing, it has to come from those at the bottom." Hermann Bellinghausen, "Interview with Subcomandante Marcos: The Ruling Class and the System Don't Have a Solution (part III)," *The Narco News Bulletin* Issue no. 41 (May 23, 2006).

36. Neither the Zapatistas nor the UNAM students began their movements with any substantial understanding of how sexual minorities lived their struggle for survival.

3. A Duty to Intervene

1. Fanon, *Wretched of the Earth*, 38.

2. Peter Takirambudde, "Building the Record of Human Rights Violations in Africa — the Functions of Monitoring, Investigation and Advocacy," in *Effective Strategies for Protecting Human Rights: Prevention and Intervention, Trade and Education,* ed. David Barnhizer (Burlington, Vt.: Ashgate Press, 2001).

3. For an excellent account of the institutional history of human rights NGOs, see Yves Dezalay and Bryant Garth, *The Internationalization of Palace Wars: Lawyers, Economists, and the Contest to Transform Latin American States* (Chicago: University of Chicago Press, 2002).

4. Roger Kaplan (primary author) and the International Council on Human Rights Policy, *Journalism, Media and the Challenge of Human Rights Reporting* (Versoix, Switzerland: ICHRP, 2002), 106.

5. George Alagiah, "A Necessary Intrusion," *Independent* (London), August 23, 1992.

6. Kay Schaffer and Sidonie Smith, *Human Rights and Narrated Lives: The Ethics of Recognition* (New York: Palgrave Macmillan, 2004), 24.

7. In a related vein, cultural theorist Allen Feldman argues that "the dissemination of biographies and testimonies of political terror ... traverses a terrain of legibility and credibility that must be considered part and parcel of the cultural construction of human rights practices in our times." Allen Feldman, "Memory Theaters, Virtual Witnessing, and the Trauma-Aesthetic," *Biography* 27, no. 1 (Winter 2004): 163–64.

8. Ibid., 163–202.

9. The character of Paul Rusesabagina is played by Don Cheadle, and Colonel Oliver is played by Nick Nolte. The Rusesabagina character was based on an actual person and Colonel Oliver was supposed to be a composite figure made up of numerous UN officials. Director Terry George originally tried to get Denzel Washington and later Will Smith to play the part of Rusesabagina but was unsuccessful. He believed, correctly, that he needed a star like one of these two men in order to sell the script to a Hollywood studio. When Hollywood interests rejected the film, George was forced to go elsewhere, ultimately receiving funding from the governments of South Africa and Italy in a joint partnership venture.

10. In interviews about the film included as extra features on the DVD, George has expressed quite clearly that the original screenplay, written by Kier Pearson, was comprised of a multiplicity of characters with no particular character performing the role of central protagonist. It was, then, George's decision to focus on Paul Rusesabagina and his heroic attempts to save his family and those trapped in the hotel. In Pearson's words, "he [Terry George] wanted to tailor the script. . . . In my original draft, it was written more like *Traffic*. Paul was the main character but there was a number of supporting characters in there, and he said, 'Hey, look, we need to pare this down; we need to focus more on Paul and Tatiana, so that people will come . . . for anything else because of the love story. I want to make it universal. I want to reach a wide audience.' "

11. Quote from "A Message of Peace: Making Hotel Rwanda," produced and directed by Greg Carson for MGM Home Entertainment (2005). I have relied heavily on this interview with George because in it he provides a fairly candid account of his strategic decision-making process when making the film. The interview is part of the supplementary materials that accompany the DVD version of the film.

12. Interview with Terry George, Greg Carson, "Message."

13. George's expressed interest in making a film about Africa, and thus to move away from his more familiar cinematic terrain of Ireland, suggests that his critical intervention was directed, at least in part, toward redressing the relative invisibility of violence in the global South on an international stage.

14. Interview with Terry George, Carson, "Message."

15. Feldman, "Memory Theaters, Virtual Witnessing, and the Trauma-Aesthetic," 169.

16. Interview with Paul Rusesabagina, Carson, "Message."

17. As the moment of evacuation nears the nearly all white faces on the buses stare out the windows at the Rwandans gathered at the entrance to the hotel. One foreigner is seen taking a snapshot of the guests, who one supposes, are not likely to survive once the foreigners depart. The

racial logic of rescuer, rescued, and victim is underscored by the director, who redoubles the moment in the filmic rendering through the act of
photographic recording.

18. Interview with Terry George, Carson, "Message."

19. In the words of one otherwise critical review: "Credit where credit's
due: Terry George's atrocity-docudrama *Hotel Rwanda* addresses that
nation's 1994 firestorm of civilian massacre without somehow contriving
to place a white man at center stage." Michael Atkinson, "Cheadle Survives
a Timid Account of the Rwandan Genocide," *Village Voice,* December 21,
2004.

20. As the actor Don Cheadle unwittingly does when he uses his *Hotel
Rwanda* notoriety to lobby for U.S. intervention in Darfur. For the dangers
lurking behind this genuinely humanitarian impulse one need only recall
that Pentagon generals told Wesley Clark that in the wake of 9/11 the
Bush administration had a "five-year campaign plan" to attack not only
Afghanistan but "Iraq, Syria, Lebanon, Iran, Libya, Sudan and Somalia."
For an account of the incredible degree of sanctioned ignorance behind
calls for U.S. intervention, see Gary Leupp's " 'Out of Iraq, into Darfur'?
Just Saying No to Imperialist Intervention," *Z magazine,* May 11, 2006.

21. Michael Taussig, *Shamanism, Colonialism and the Wild Man: A
Study in Terror and Healing* (Chicago: Chicago University Press, 1986).

22. Feldman, "Memory Theaters, Virtual Witnessing, and the Trauma-
Aesthetic," 197.

23. Richard Porton, "Collective Guilt and Individual Responsibility: An
Interview with Michael Haneke," *Cineaste* 31, no. 1 (Winter 2005): 50.

24. *Battle of Algiers,* director Gillo Pontecorvo, Casbah Films, 1966.

25. *Drowning by Bullets,* directors Philip Brooks and Alan Hayling, First
Run/Icarus Films, 1992.

26. Cited in "Michael Haneke," Mattias Frey, *Senses of Cinema* (August
2003).

27. Again, the move from public to private space is critical to Haneke's
exposure of how this ideological boundary is used by the bourgeoisie to
try to hide any complicit entanglement with historical violence. Haneke's
relentless assault on the refuge of the private is both amusing and trenchant.

28. Schaffer and Smith, *Human Rights and Narrated Lives,* 232.

29. For example, in May 2008 the Western media was vociferously
aghast at what they called the refusal of the Burmese military government to
allow UN aid workers into the country following the devastations wrought
by Cyclone Nargis, which resulted in more than a hundred thousand deaths.
As four U.S. naval ships assembled in the Gulf of Thailand off the coast of
Myanmar, including the destroyer USS *Mustin* and the three amphibious
assault ships, the USS *Essex,* the USS *Juneau,* and the USS *Harpers Ferry,*
reporters asked U.S. Defense Secretary Robert Gates if the reluctance of
Burma's leaders to accept aid might be a consequence of their suspicions

about U.S. military intentions. Gates rejected the suggestion saying that "I'd be surprised if they misinterpreted our intentions that badly." Adding that "our interest here is totally nonpolitical." The sense of moral outrage from the West reached such a fevered pitch that a week later the French government called upon the UN General Assembly to authorize aid intervention irrespective of whether the Burmese government would allow it. But we should be clear about the details of this oft-reported refusal. At no time did the Myanmar government refuse aid or even aid workers wholly. Relief help from China, Japan, and Indonesia, for example, was accepted and activated immediately. What is true is that the Myanmar government was reluctant to accept aid and aid workers, especially from the United States and the UK, given both the long colonial history of intervention and the more recent aggressions led by the United States — in the form of trade and investment bans — and because the Myanmar government was insistent about regulating the flow of aid workers into the country — a condition largely unacceptable to the West. Now I raise this not as a way of defending the Myanmar military rulers for their own domestic record of attending to the plight of the Myanmarian poor before or following the recent natural disaster. However, what I want to insist upon is that their so-called suspicion about the humanitarian concern of the West, which was scripted here as the product of excessive paranoia, was not so ridiculous or so implausible as to be beyond the pale of comprehension. In fact, such a rejection is not at all unprecedented.

In the wake of Hurricane Katrina, fifty-nine countries offered aid to the United States, including Cuba, which offered to send sixteen hundred medics, eighty-three tons of medical supplies and a number of mobile field hospitals. Venezuela also offered to send 1 million barrels of gasoline, some $5 million in disaster aid and a team of two hundred humanitarian aid workers. Both offers were summarily rejected by the Bush administration. In response to Cuba's offer White House spokesman Scott McClellan gave this reply: "When it comes to Cuba, we have one message for Fidel Castro: He needs to offer the people of Cuba their freedom." Now for anyone who has followed the U.S. government relief effort along the southern gulf coast, it is quite evident that FEMA certainly could have used some help, both in the immediate wake of the crisis and on in to today. For two excellent accounts of the paradoxes of international relief efforts more generally, see Alex de Waal, *Famine Crimes: Politics and the Disaster Relief Industry in Africa* (African Rights and the International African Institute in association with Indiana University Press, 1997) and Fiona Terry, *Condemned to Repeat: The Paradox of Humanitarian Action* (Ithaca: Cornell University Press, 2002).

30. Said, "Nationalism, Human Rights, and Interpretation," 55.

31. For solid critiques of the humanitarian mission in Bosnia, see Noam Chomsky, *The New Military Humanism: Lessons from Kosovo* (Monroe,

Maine: Common Courage Press, 1999); Diana Johnstone, *Fool's Crusade: Yugoslavia, NATO, and Western Delusions* (New York: Monthly Review Press, 2003); and Edward S. Herman and David Peterson, "The Dismantling of Yugoslavia: A Study in Inhumanitarian Intervention (and a Western Liberal-Left Intellectual and Moral Collapse)," *Monthly Review* 59, no. 5 (October 2007): 1–62.

32. Power is a human rights lawyer, journalist, and founding executive director of Harvard University's Carr Center for Human Rights Policy. She recently served as the top foreign policy advisor to Barack Obama during his presidential campaign, until her sudden dismissal for calling his campaign opponent, Hillary Clinton, a "monster."

33. Samantha Power, *A Problem from Hell: America and the Age of Genocide* (New York: Basic Books, 2002) 504.

34. Samantha Power, "Raising the Cost of Genocide," *Dissent* (Spring 2002): 94.

35. Ibid.

36. Amin, *Beyond U.S. Hegemony?* 10.

37. Ibid., 12.

38. Chalmers Johnson, "America's Empire of Bases," www.TomDispatch.com (January 15, 2004).

4. Expiation for the Dispossessed

1. As far as I know, these lectures have not yet been published. The quotation is from my notes while in attendance at the series of three lectures delivered by Balibar ("On Politics and History: Presence, Cruelty, and the Universals"). In schematic form this conversion process has a dual structure: on the one hand, the violence of territorial expansion/state formation must be converted into legality while, at the same time, and through the same process, the violence of resistance is converted into illegality. Nonconvertibility would then mark the failures, gaps, inadequacies, and fissures in this state project. It is imperative to bear in mind, however, that this process does not end with the state monopolization over the means of violence; rather it is a necessary process for the maintenance and reproduction of such a monopoly and for the state itself. This is the upshot of Benjamin's deconstruction of the distinction between law-making and law-preserving in "Critique of Violence." For a superb reading of Benjamin's analysis, see David Lloyd's "Rage against the Divine," *South Atlantic Quarterly* 102, no. 2 (Spring 2007): 345–72.

2. In their genealogy of the relation between culture and the state, David Lloyd and Paul Thomas show that the theory of representation is remarkably internally consistent across state institutions (from political representation to biographical representation) and that it is what "connects distinct institutions of bourgeois political culture." Lloyd and Thomas, *Culture and the State,* 6. Indeed Lloyd has argued more recently that the

traditional conceptual hierarchy that places culture and representation as subordinate to and derivative of the state's monopoly on violence may need to be reversed insofar as representation serves as the conditions of possibility for representative democracy to emerge. See David Lloyd, "Representation's Coup," in Swati Chattopadhyay and Bhaskar Sarkar, eds., *The Subaltern and the Popular* (London: Routledge, forthcoming).

3. Nicos Poulantzas, *State, Power, Socialism,* 77.

4. Ibid., 76.

5. Richard Soloman, "Preface," *Transitional Justice: How Emerging Democracies Reckon with Former Regimes,* ed. Neil Kritz, vol. 2 (Washington, D.C: United States Institute of Peace 1995), xxiii.

6. Again, advocates suggest, such redressive and curative functions of the Truth Commission are largely absent from the determinations of guilt and innocence in the juridical form of the trial. As Allen Feldman argues, however, this is a problematic orientation: "Following a redressive and curative trajectory, human rights frameworks and quasi-medicalized tropes of trauma circulate and archive the experiences of terror and abuse as episodes scheduled for eventual overcoming through redemptive survival, recovery, and restorative justice. Does this prescriptive plotting 'archaicize' terror, creating museums of suffering?" Feldman, "Memory Theaters, Virtual Witnessing, and the Trauma-Aesthetic," 165.

7. Joseph Slaughter, "A Question of Narration: The Voice in International Human Rights Law," *Human Rights Quarterly* 19, no. 2 (1997): 415–16.

8. Preamble, Universal Declaration of Human Rights, adopted December 10, 1948.

9. For excellent accounts on the politics of *testimonios,* see Rosaura Sánchez, *Telling Identities: The Californio Testimonios* (Minneapolis: University of Minnesota Press, 1995), and John Beverley's *Against Literature* (Minneapolis: University of Minnesota Press, 1993).

10. Barbara Harlow, *Barred: Women, Writing, and Political Detention,* 252–53. On the *bildungsroman* see, M. M. Bakhtin, "The Bildungsroman and Its Significance in the History of Realism," in *Speech Genres and Other Late Essays* (Austin: University of Texas Press, 1986).

11. Feldman, "Memory Theaters, Virtual Witnessing, and the Trauma-Aesthetic," 173.

12. David Atwell and Barbara Harlow, "Introduction: South African Fiction after Apartheid," *Modern Fiction Studies* 46, no. 1 (2000): 3.

13. Feldman, "Memory Theaters, Virtual Witnessing, and the Trauma-Aesthetic," 164. An ironic locus, to say the least, given that "part and parcel of the mutation of the state into an apparatus for chronic violence are the very institutional rationalities of law, medicine, and psychology that are *ex post facto* expected to provide redress and therapeusis in their adaptation and cooptation of the post-terror biographical artifact" (168).

14. Jeremy Cronin, "A Luta Discontinua? The TRC Final Report and the Nation Building Project," paper presented at University of the Witwatersrand, June 1999. Cited in Atwell and Harlow, "Introduction," 4.

15. In the simplest sense the Greek term *catechresis,* which Gayatri Spivak has recently revived, designates the act by which something is misnamed because there is no name for it. See Spivak, *A Critique of Postcolonial Reason: Toward a History of the Vanishing Present* (Cambridge, Mass.: Harvard University Press, 1999).

16. Étienne Balibar, "Violence, Ideality and Cruelty," in *Politics and the Other Scene,* trans. Christine Jones, James Swenson, and Chris Turner (London: Verso 2002), 145.

17. Ibid., 129.

18. Ibid., xi–xii.

19. See, e.g., Rama Mani, *Beyond Retribution: Seeking Justice in the Shadows of War* (Cambridge: Polity Press, 2002); Andrew Schapp, *Political Reconciliation* (London: Routledge, 2005); and the later work of Priscilla Hayner such as her essay "International Guidelines for the Creation and Operation of Truth Commissions: A Preliminary Proposal," *Law and Contemporary Problems* 59, no. 4 (1996): 168–75.

20. As Jacques Derrida has suggested, Truth Commissions and other forms of international judicialism may contribute to the generalized crises in international law that actually helps to generate a "new international" that "already denounces the limits of a discourse on human rights that will remain inadequate, sometimes hypocritical, and in any case formalistic and inconsistent with itself as long as the law of the market, the 'foreign debt,' the inequality of techno-scientific, military, and economic development maintain an effective inequality as monstrous as that which prevails today, to a greater extent than ever in the history of humanity." Derrida, *Spectres of Marx,* 85.

21. Feldman, "Memory Theaters, Virtual Witnessing, and the Trauma-Aesthetic," 170.

22. Nelly Richard, *Cultural Residues: Chile in Transition,* trans. Alan West-Durán and Theodore Quester (Minneapolis: University of Minnesota Press, 2004), 15.

23. In the briefest of outlines and with only those details most immediately relevant to my analysis in this chapter, Pinochet's rise and rule ran as follows: On August 23, 1973, Chilean President Salvador Allende named Augusto Pinochet Ugarte commander-in-chief of the army. In the midst of mounting turmoil from within and outside the country, General Pinochet had pledged his eternal loyalty to both the president and to democracy. Less than three weeks later, on September 11, 1973, General Pinochet led a bloody coup d'état. Tens of thousands of leftists were killed and/or disappeared during and after the coup, and thousands more (including Dorfman) fled the country soon thereafter. According to human rights reports more

than 180,000 people were detained in the first year of the dictatorship, an estimated 90 percent of them tortured. His dictatorial rule over the country would last until March 12, 1990 following his defeat in a plebiscite a year earlier.

24. Ariel Dorfman, *Death and the Maiden* (New York: Penguin, 1992).

25. Ariel Dorfman, *La muerte y la doncella* (New York: Siete Cuentos Editorial, 2001).

26. September 11, 1991, marks the eighteenth anniversary of the coup d'état that resulted in President Salvador Allende's suicide and General Pinochet's coming to power. Dorfman, "Afterword," 71–75.

27. Ibid., 72.

28. As Dorfman has written in a more recent work in the wake of Pinochet's arrest in London (October 1998), utilizing a mode of direct address to speak to Pinochet: "We couldn't, given the terms of the transaction we agreed to under the specter of your guns, express our true emotions, fearful that if you didn't like our latest move you would just up and kick the table on which the game was being played, shoot the player who had dared to trump your card. We got democracy back, General, but you set limits of how far and deep that democracy could go." Ariel Dorfman, *Exorcising Terror: The Incredible Unending Trial of General Augusto Pinochet* (New York: Seven Stories Press, 2002), 28.

29. Dorfman, "Afterword," 72.

30. Dorfman, *Death and the Maiden*, Act I, Scene I, 9.

31. Idelber Avelar, "From Plato to Pinochet: Torture, Confession, and the History of Truth," *The Letter of Violence: Essays on Narrative, Ethics, and Politics* (New York: Palgrave Macmillan, 2004), 42–43.

32. It may be the case that the film does this to a much greater degree than the play; however, what Avelar says about the film is applicable to the play, insofar as the differences between the two — at least on the points he focuses — are minimal.

33. Dorfman, *Death and the Maiden*, Act III, Scene I, 66.

34. Dorfman, *Exorcising Terror*, 48.

35. A fuller rendering of the quotation runs as follows: "The sensation of a monotonous lack of distinction and contrast in the ensemble of social idioms, political slogans, communicative exchanges, vital modulations, and subjective expressions derives from a 'consensus achieved forcibly by formalized politics [that] creates a plane resistant to any excitement or enthusiasm' while installing the predictable, the foreseeable, as a unique horizon in the fulfillment of meaning. There are various reasons that coincide in the leveling formation of this plane, beginning with the ideological loss of all that, in the past, sounded like promise or utopia is now replaced by mechanisms, procedures, and results that speak the resigned language of calculation in order to better serve the new equation of democratic realism.... Center is its name; this does not designate a party among

others, but instead the generic name of a new configuration of political space, a free unfolding of consensual power that corresponds to the free apolitical development of production and circulation. The 'center' is no longer the center, nor an indeterminate point that might control the threatening disequilibriums of extreme positions, but instead is a diffuse, vast and equilibrated territory where what rules, almost without obstacles, is the average: that which adjusts itself — in form and proportion — to the rule of not disrupting the social ranks, of not departing from the script, of not losing the composure of democratic order that is now reduced to an airy syntax of contractual arrangements stripped of all shadow of malaise or indignation.

"The center, the 'center function' and its dominant representations (common sense, practical reason, the laws of the market: the force of the facts), produces the rotation of images of political, social, and economic stability around this unifying paradigm that shows us that maturity is common sense, common sense is moderation, and moderation means being resigned to the consensus and the market." Richard, *Cultural Residues,* 146.

36. Balibar, *Politics and the Other Scene,* 145.

37. Anastasio Somoza García was the son of a wealthy coffee planter. He was sent to Philadelphia to attend the Pierce School of Business Administration, where he met and married Salvadora Debayle Sacasa, a member of one of Nicaragua's wealthiest families. In 1926, upon his return from the United States, Somoza García joined the Liberal rebellion in support of the presidential claims of Juan Sacasa, his wife's uncle.

38. Claribel Alegría and Darwin Flakoll, *Death of Somoza: The First Person Story of the Guerrillas Who Assassinated the Nicaraguan Dictator* (Willimantic, Conn.: Curbstone Press, 1996), 2–3.

39. Ibid., 7. For Somoza's claims for the historical record, see the rather delusional text *Nicaragua Betrayed.* It is quite likely, in the wake of the Iranian hostage crisis and the central role that the shah of Iran's exile in the United States had played, that Carter was not interested in hosting another dictator, particularly one who was no longer of any use as an anticommunist client.

40. General Stroessner ruled Paraguay for thirty-five years, from 1954 to 1989. In 1992 in a police station in the capital city of Asunción, investigators discovered what has become known as the "terror archives." In these buried documents were recorded the fates of thousands of Latin Americans who had been secretly kidnapped, tortured, and killed by security forces organized by the dictators of the Southern Cone.

41. Alegría and Flakoll, *Death of Somoza,* 7.

42. Medieval intellectual advocates would include such notable theological figures as Aquinas, Bodin, and Mariana to name but very few out of a long list of possible entries.

43. Alegría and Flakoll, *Death of Somoza,* "Preface."

44. For an excellent account of this transposition of/to the literature of crime, see Michel Foucault's *Discipline and Punish: The Birth of the Prison*, trans. Alan Sheridan (New York: Vintage Books, 1979). And for a superb account of how criminality has been used to create divisions among the laboring poor (as well as how the laboring poor and their criminals have defied such attempts), see Linebaugh, *The London Hanged*.

45. Alegría and Flakoll, "Preface."

46. As Feldman says: "These narratives of human rights violation are testimonials to the irreconcilable. They neither refract a unified speaking subject, nor readily lend themselves to unification and instrumentation from without, despite the many orderings and reductions applied to them by law, media and medicine. Asymmetric subject positions are not only figures within the narrative, but also are relationships inscribed into the symbolic economy of narrative transmission, response, and adjudication. The authoritative and monophonic application of a narrative closure can only instigate further asymmetric subject positions, further tales left untold, further forms of cultural violence, and further inequitable regimes of truth obtained from the condition of those who have been othered by violence." Feldman, "Memory Theaters, Virtual Witnessing, and the Trauma-Aesthetic," 194.

5. Combat Theory

1. Eqbal Ahmad, "The Making of *The Battle of Algiers*," *The Selected Writings of Eqbal Ahmad* (New York: Columbia University Press, 2006), 88.

2. Ibid., 88–89.

3. Frantz Fanon, *The Wretched of the Earth*, trans. Richard Philcox (New York: Grove Press, 2004).

4. Ibid., 236.

5. In *Culture and Imperialism* (New York: Penguin Books, 2000), Said correctly treats this as a new world-historic situation distinct from pre–World War II revolutionary movements. As he writes: "The militant groups between the two world wars were not clearly or completely anti-West. Some believed that relief from colonialism could come by working with Christianity; others believed that westernization was the solution. In Africa these between-the-wars efforts were represented ... by such people as Herbert Macaulay, Leopold Senghor, J. H. Casely Hayford, Samuel Ahuma; in the Arab world during this period Saad Zaghloul, Nuri as-Said, Bishara al-Khoury were counterparts. Even later revolutionary leaders — Ho Chi Minh in Vietnam for example — originally held the view that aspects of Western culture could be helpful in ending colonialism" (196). Soon after the war, however, as Fanon would write, "Today the third world ... faces Europe like a colossal mass whose aim should be to try to resolve the problems to which Europe has not been able to find the answers." Fanon, *Wretched of the Earth*, 314.

6. Fanon, *Wretched of the Earth*, 237. The referent here is, I believe, intentionally left unclear. Is he referring to the whole humanist tradition? To Rousseau? To Marx? Who knows? The fact that we do not know suggests that he is not referring to any specific formulations, but rather to the gap between ideas and revolutionary practice and how the contradictions between the ideal and the material have worked against the possibility of actualization. Consequently, the praxis of emancipation must be wholly refigured.

7. Including apparently, what had been the most enlightened of Western theorizations and movements, Lenin and the Bolshevik Revolution.

8. Samira Kawash, "Terrorists and Vampires: Fanon's Spectral Violence of Decolonization," in *Frantz Fanon: Critical Perspectives*, ed. Anthony Alessandrini (New York: Routledge, 1999), 237.

9. Michel Foucault, *The History of Sexuality*, vol. 1: *An Introduction*, trans. Robert Hurley (New York: Vintage Books, 1980), 94. Foucault, it should be noted, while occasionally using the French terms "violence" and "power" interchangeably, does distinguish the two concept words. As Thomas Flynn has argued, Foucault's model seems to suggest that while "all violence attaches to relations of power, not all relations of power necessarily entail violence." Rather, he says, "it is with that species of power which Foucault calls 'domination' and which we might label 'negative' power that violence seems necessarily associated." At the same time, Flynn acknowledges that "it is not easy to separate them in practice" either for Foucault or for us, "whether it be the 'quiet violence' of psychoanalysis, the 'instinctive violence' of knowledge or simply the violence that attends to our apparently consensual agreements, violence, insofar as it entails 'action on the action of others' seems ingredient in the very exercise of power." Thomas R. Flynn, *Sartre, Foucault and Historical Reason: A Poststructuralist Mapping of History*, vol. 2 (Chicago: University of Chicago Press, 2005), 244–45.

10. Fanon, *Wretched of the Earth*, 40. This is, of course, not the only major theoretical difference between Fanon and Foucault with respect to their modelings of power. Foucault's erasure of the state is probably the most significant difference from Fanon's model. Nevertheless, the conception of power that Foucault develops has strong affinities with that articulated in Fanon's account of violence in the colonial world.

11. Achille Mbembe, "Necropolitics," *Public Culture* 15, no. 1 (2003): 24.

12. Ibid., 24.

13. Frantz Fanon, *Black Skin, White Masks* (New York: Grove Press, 1967), 220. To this tragicomic account he added the footnote that "what [the master] wants from the slave is not recognition but work" (220, fn. 8).

14. Despite the identification of *Black Skin, White Masks* as Fanon's "most psychoanalytic text" (Kobena Mercer), it is important to recognize

that Fanon's version of psychoanalysis was never enclosed by the psychoanalytic scene or the pathological subject.

15. Pheng Cheah has very usefully articulated this dilemma: "instead of regarding the inhuman as an attribute, effect, or consequence of the global capitalist system *qua* product of alienation from our humanity, it would be more accurate to situate global capitalism as the terminal form of microphysical and biopolitical technologies, tactics, and strategies that stretch across labor-exporting and receiving nations.... What is at work here, however, is a form of inhuman production that cannot be regulated and transcended because it is the condition of possibility of humanity.... We can call this 'the inhuman' in the general sense, a form of inhumanity that is not secondary to or derived from the human because humanity itself is its product-effect." Cheah, *Inhuman Conditions*, 231.

16. Fanon, *Wretched of the Earth*, 4.

17. Mbembe, "Necropolitics," 25–26. Or again, as Fanon said of colonial territorialization: "There is no occupation of territory, on the one hand, and independence of persons on the other. It is the country as a whole, its history, its daily pulsation that are contested, disfigured, in the hope of definitive annihilation. Under this condition, the individual's breathing is an observed, an occupied breathing. It is a combat breathing." Frantz Fanon, "Algeria Unveiled," *A Dying Colonialism*, trans. Haakon Chevalier (New York: Grove Press, 1965), 65.

18. Fanon, *Wretched of the Earth*, 93.

19. Ibid., 41.

20. David Lloyd advances this argument with respect to the "subaltern" when he writes: "Every approach to the subaltern seems to be haunted with the specter of violence. This violence that associates with the subaltern exceeds the empirical record of peasant insurrections and riots through which subaltern groups explode into the historical archive as it exceeds the record of state violence directed at the subaltern.... What haunts the concept is not the violence done by or to the subaltern, but rather something intrinsically categorical, the violence of the subaltern, we might say, or, indeed, the subaltern as violence." David Lloyd, "Representation's Coup."

21. Cheah, *Inhuman Conditions*, 17. There are, of course, countertendencies in the West, as in Said's exemplary account in *Culture and Imperialism* and Benita Parry's *Postcolonial Studies: A Materialist Critique* (New York: Routledge, 2004). And Fanon's intellectual death here is not widely eulogized elsewhere.

22. Cheah, *Inhuman Conditions*, 18.

23. Alexander defines the neocolonial state formation as made up of "those states that emerged from the colonial 'order' as the forfeiters to nationalist claims to sovereignty and autonomy." She defines the neoimperial state formation as comprised of "those advanced capitalist states that are the dominant partners in the global 'order.'" She does not, quite

correctly, attempt to organize these forms in terms of a linear temporality, thereby preventing the misapprehension of these shifting state and social formations as constituting an absolute break with modernity's imperial or colonial pasts. Alexander, *Pedagogies of Crossing*, 4.

24. The concept of "palimpsestic time" that Alexander develops is particularly useful for any contemporary critical project that rejects the linear temporality of modernity. As Alexander writes, "The idea of the 'new' structured through the 'old' scrambled, palimpsestic character of time, both jettisons the truncated distance of linear time and dislodges the impulse for incommensurability, which the ideology of distance creates. It thus rescrambles the 'here and now' and the 'then and there' to a 'here and there' and a 'then and now,' and makes visible what Payal Banerjee calls the ideological traffic between and among formations that are otherwise positioned as dissimilar." Alexander, *Pedagogies of Crossing*, 190.

25. There are of course many works that have taken aim at the tendentiousness of Western models of development, but I want to mention two here that together form a useful way into examining the relation between development and theory. See the classic text on development by Walter Rodney, *How Europe Underdeveloped Africa* (Washington, D.C.: Howard University Press, 1972) and the incisive critique of metropolitan theory in Aijaz Ahmad, *In Theory: Classes, Nations, Literatures* (New York: Verso, 1992).

26. Zolo, *Cosmopolis*, 27. U.S. liberal-left intellectual Michael Walzer went further, declaring that "judging the war from an ethical point of view, it is impossible to imagine a more nobler cause or a more infamous enemy." Zolo, *Cosmopolis*, 47 n.27.

27. This, too, met with glorious praise as Western leaders clamored to announce a new era in international relations. British Prime Minister Blair declared that "we are fighting for new values," for "a new internationalism where the brutal repression of whole ethnic groups will no longer be tolerated." German Foreign Minister Fischer echoed the German intellectual Ulrich Beck's declaration of a "new military humanism." And U.S. Secretary of State Madeleine Albright claimed that "the defense of human rights is a form of mission." Despite the high-sounding principles and values, "the New Humanism" of the Clinton doctrine sounded pretty much like "the old imperialism" save for the absence of a superpower competitor, as National Security Advisor Anthony Lake described the new situation: "Throughout the Cold War we contained a global threat to market democracies," but now we can move on to "consolidate the victory of democracy and open markets." Chomsky, *The New Military Humanism*, 14.

28. Balibar, *We, the People of Europe?* 131.

29. For good recent critiques of this narrative of revolutionary failure, see Antonio Negri, *Goodbye Mr. Socialism* (New York: Seven Stories Press, 2008), and Amin, *The World We Wish to See*.

30. This drive for an alternative form of human rights includes the development of what Upendra Baxi correctly describes as a "market-friendly paradigm of human rights, which takes the form of full reassertion of the UDHR paradigm in relation to corporate governance and business conduct." Upendra Baxi, *The Future of Human Rights,* 2nd ed. (Oxford: Oxford University Press, 2006), 276. For an appalling example of this development, see Afua Hirsch, "Do Hedge Funds Have Human Rights?" *Guardian,* UK (January 28, 2009).

31. Mbembe, "Necropolitics," 14.

32. There are of course numerous others, many of excellent quality, but these particular works have played a particularly important role in the development of ideas put forth in this book. Zolo, *Cosmopolis;* Cheah, *Inhuman Conditions;* Rajagopal, *International Law from Below;* Miéville, *Between Equal Rights;* Alexander, *Pedagogies of Crossing.*

33. The starting point, then, tends to be one of a general unquestioned faith in the cosmopolitan model as the only possible response to the very real crisis of the statist Westphalian world order. Given this assumption, the actual historical record of the various cosmopolitical attempts tends to be downplayed or ignored in favor of trying to advance the technical means of improving and reforming existing international institutions.

34. Zolo, *Cosmopolis,* 15. This is not to say that these theorists do not come to the conclusion that, as Zolo says, "some form of *pactum subjectionis,* subordinating the power of self-defense of states to the control of an appropriately armed central authority, appears to be indispensable" (x). Rather it is to emphasize that this is not their starting point and that this fact carries important political and epistemological consequences.

35. Ibid., 2.

36. Ibid., 13.

37. As Samir Amin has written, this dominant form of internationalism has been persistently challenged by a countergenealogy of "the internationalism of peoples." This alternative internationalism began, according to Amin, with the formation of the First International in 1864, ran through the Fourth International, and ultimately concluded with the Bandung system and the first globalization of struggles (1955–80). The Bandung era, he argues, "was brought to a close by the neoliberal offensive of the oligopolies of the imperialist center (the triad: the United States, Europe, Japan)." Amin, *The World We Wish to See,* 11–16.

38. Peter Fitzpatrick, " 'Gods Would Be Needed...': American Empire and the Rule of (International) Law," *Leiden Journal of International Law* 16, no. 3 (2003): 466.

39. As international legal theorist Anthony Carty wrote a little over a decade ago: "A very major deficiency in the doctrinal analysis of international law is that no systematic undertaking is usually offered of the

influence of colonialism in the development of the basic conceptual frame-work of the subject." It is this lacuna within the study of international law that a few theorists have begun to critically redress. Anthony Carty, *Was Ireland Conquered? International Law and the Irish Question* (London: Pluto Press, 1996).

40. Miéville, *Between Equal Rights*, 303.

41. Ibid., 304.

42. Additionally, in a critical distinction between international and domestic law, Miéville astutely notes that in the case of international law "the struggle over the legal form is far more mediated" than it is in domestic law: "States, not classes or other social forces, are the fundamental contend-ing agents of international law, and while their claims and counterclaims are informed by their own domestic class struggles, they do not 'represent' classes in any direct way. It is generally the opposing ruling classes of dif-ferent states that clash with the legal form, each with its own class agenda. These internecine battles between the 'warring brothers' of the ruling class make up the great swathe of the international legal structure, and in them there is little purchase for a fundamentally progressive, subversive or radical legal position" (317).

Coda

1. Hendrik Hertzberg, "Smart Power," *New Yorker,* January 26, 2009.

2. www.asil.org/il08/clinton.ht

3. Nossel coined the phrase in 2004. Suzanne Nossel, "Smart Power," *Foreign Affairs* (March–April 2004): 131–42. The more recent Nossel quote is from Hertzberg, "Smart Power."

4. In 2002, the Germany-based Bertelsmann Company admitted that they had lied about their ties to the Nazi party, which included making profits from slave labor and publishing propaganda. The revelations about Bertelsmann's sordid past came to light during their successful attempt to take over the publishing giant Random House in 1998 as Bertels-mann rewrote the company's history in order to avoid troubling the deal. "Bertelsmann Admits Nazi Past," *BBC* (October 8, 2002).

5. Nossel, "Smart Power," 132.

6. Obama, "Torture and Secrecy Betray Core American Values," Octo-ber 4, 2007. Online at www.barackobama.com/2007/10/04/obama_torture _and_secrecy_betr.php.

7. From August 2008 to January 2009 the United States launched thirty-eight missile strikes inside Pakistan killing an estimated 132 people.

8. Tom Hayden, "CIA Secret Rendition Policy Backed by Human Rights Groups?" *Huffington Post* (February 1, 2009).

9. Popular opposition to U.S. renditions emerged in earnest in Italy in 2003 when it came to light that the CIA, with full knowledge and cooperation from the Berlusconi government, abducted an Egyptian cleric

who was flown to Egypt and tortured. And then, shortly after the cleric's abduction, another story followed in which "an Egyptian citizen, Khalid Masri, was grabbed by men wearing ski masks, stripped, blindfolded, placed in diapers, shackled and flown from Macedonia to Albania. He was released five months later as a case of mistaken identity." (Hayden, "CIA Secret Rendition Policy Backed by Human Rights Groups?") The European Parliament subsequently condemned renditions as "an illegal instrument used by the United States." Greg Miller, "Obama Preserves Renditions as Counter-Terrorism Tool," *Los Angeles Times,* February 1, 2009.

10. Anonymous Obama administration official, quoted in Greg Miller's "Obama Preserves Renditions as Counter-Terrorism Tool." As in this account, it should be clear that no action is ever undertaken by the supra-colonial state without first going through an extensive legal vetting process. In the crucial but complex cases, this process is engaged not in order to determine the legality or illegality of a particular course of action, but rather its legalizability (a category most easily defined as the "not-illegal").

11. Tom Malinkowski, cited in "Obama Lets CIA Keep Controversial Renditions Tool," Greg Miller, *Chicago Tribune,* January 31, 2009.

12. A good example of liberal shock at the "abuse" of human rights can be found in Afua Hirsch's, "Do Hedge Funds Have Human Rights?" *Guardian* (UK), January 28, 2009. After the lawyers for two large hedge funds (RAB Special Situations and SRM Global Master Fund) argued in a British court that the 2008 nationalization of the British bank Northern Rock amounted to a violation of their human rights under the first proto-col of the European Convention on Human Rights, Hirsch mused: "There seems to be something deeply counter-intuitive about this incarnation of human rights claims, rooted not in protecting such sacred freedoms as the right to life or a private and family life, but mitigating loss of profits." In contrast to Hirsch's liberal apoplexy, however, human rights historian Upendra Baxi actually anticipated this type of development in the closing chapter of his book *The Future of Human Rights,* 2nd ed. (Oxford: Oxford University Press, 2006). At that time Baxi was already exploring resistance strategies "to the onset of the trade-related, market-friendly paradigm of human rights, which takes the form of full reassertion of the UDHR para-digm in relation to corporate governance and business conduct" (276). Baxi was not at all surprised by these developments within human rights, given that any nonidealized account of human rights has long had to reckon with the fact that the concept of human rights is extraordinarily broad and subject to virtually unlimited appropriation.

13. It should be pointed out, as a curious fact of no small import, that the articulation of "our" imperial interests *in the frame of the inter-national* continues to be cast in the older language of nationalism, as under the terms and conditions of "our laws and constitution" and "our core

values." This again gives credence to Alexander's theorization of palimpsestic time (see chapter 5), as well as underscoring the inordinate power of the supracolonial state to control the very language of "the international."

14. China Miéville, "Multilateralism as Terror: Haiti, Imperialism and (International) Law," paper delivered at the Critical Legal Conference, University of Glasgow (September 5, 2008).

15. Nossel, "Smart Power," 132.

Index

❖

Randall Williams has taught at the University of California in San Diego and in Riverside in the departments of ethnic studies, film and visual culture, and literature. He has been involved with various social movements, including ACT UP and the recently formed Teachers Against Occupation.